Cambridge Elements ≡

Elements in Criminology
edited by
David Weisburd
George Mason University and The Hebrew University of Jerusalem

A FRAMEWORK FOR ADDRESSING VIOLENCE AND SERIOUS CRIME

Focused Deterrence, Legitimacy, and Prevention

Anthony A. Braga
Northeastern University

David M. Kennedy
John Jay College of Criminal Justice, City University of New York

CAMBRIDGE
UNIVERSITY PRESS

CAMBRIDGE
UNIVERSITY PRESS

University Printing House, Cambridge CB2 8BS, United Kingdom

One Liberty Plaza, 20th Floor, New York, NY 10006, USA

477 Williamstown Road, Port Melbourne, VIC 3207, Australia

314–321, 3rd Floor, Plot 3, Splendor Forum, Jasola District Centre,
New Delhi – 110025, India

79 Anson Road, #06–04/06, Singapore 079906

Cambridge University Press is part of the University of Cambridge.

It furthers the University's mission by disseminating knowledge in the pursuit of
education, learning, and research at the highest international levels of excellence.

www.cambridge.org
Information on this title: www.cambridge.org/9781108940061
DOI: 10.1017/9781108938143

First published 2020

A catalogue record for this publication is available from the British Library.

ISBN 978-1-108-94006-1 Paperback
ISSN 2633-3341 (online)
ISSN 2633-3333 (print)

A Framework for Addressing Violence and Serious Crime

Focused Deterrence, Legitimacy, and Prevention

Elements in Criminology

DOI: 10.1017/9781108938143
First published online: November 2020

Anthony A. Braga
Northeastern University

David M. Kennedy
John Jay College of Criminal Justice, City University of New York

Author for correspondence: Anthony A. Braga, a.braga@northeastern.edu

Abstract: This Element examines an increasingly important community crime prevention strategy: focused deterrence. This strategy seeks to change offender behavior by understanding underlying crime-producing dynamics and conditions that sustain recurring crime problems, and implementing a blended set of law enforcement, community mobilization, and social service actions. The approach builds on recent theorizing on optimizing deterrence, mobilizing informal social control, enhancing police legitimacy, and reducing crime opportunities through situational crime prevention. There are three main types of focused deterrence strategies: group violence intervention programs, drug market intervention programs, and individual offender programs. A growing number of rigorous program evaluations find focused deterrence to be an effective crime prevention strategy. However, a number of steps need to be taken to ensure focused deterrence strategies are implemented properly. These steps include creating a network of capacity through partnering agencies, conducting upfront and ongoing problem analysis, and developing accountability structures and sustainability plans.

Keywords: deterrence, prevention, evidence-based policy, legitimacy, public safety

ISBNs: 9781108940061 (PB), 9781108938143 (OC)
ISSNs: 2633-3341 (online), 2633-3333 (print)

Contents

1 Introduction

Focused deterrence, sometimes called "pulling levers" policing, represents an important turning point in criminology and crime prevention practice. As will be detailed in this Element, the approach builds on theoretical insights on the proper application of deterrence principles to modify the behavior of individual and groups of high-rate offenders (Kennedy, 1997, 2008). It also draws upon new theoretical perspectives on the salience of police legitimacy and community engagement when implementing police-led crime control strategies (Braga, 2012; Kennedy, 2011). The existing empirical evidence suggests that "person focused" policing interventions associated with the standard model of policing, such as programs designed to arrest and prosecute repeat offenders, have not been effective in controlling crime (Skogan & Frydl, 2004). In contrast, a growing number of rigorous program evaluations suggest that focused deterrence strategies, designed to change offender behavior through a blended law enforcement, social service and opportunity provision, and community-based action approach, are effective in controlling crime (Weisburd & Majmundar, 2018; Braga, Weisburd, & Turchan, 2018). Anecdotal evidence along with some formal research suggest that these approaches can help improve police-community relationships in disadvantaged minority communities and reduce our reliance on arrests and mass incarceration as means to address violent crime (Brunson, 2015; Meares, 2009; Engel, Corsaro, & Ozer, 2017).

Focused deterrence follows an action research model that tailors the strategy to specific crime problems and builds upon local operational capacities to deliver sanctions and mobilize support to control high-rate offenders driving targeted problems (Braga, Kennedy, & Tita, 2002). A general theoretical reframing of deterrence has been developed (Kennedy, 1997, 2008; Kennedy, Kleiman, & Braga, 2017; Kleiman, 2009). Consistent with the problem-solving approach, three main operational variations of focused deterrence have developed: *group violence intervention* (GVI) has been applied to control violent behavior by gangs and other criminally active groups (Braga et al., 2001; McGarrell et al., 2006; Papachristos & Kirk, 2015), *drug market intervention* (DMI) has been implemented to address violence and disorder generated by overt drug markets (Kennedy, 2009a; Kennedy & Wong, 2009; Corsaro et al., 2012), and *individual offender strategies* have sought to control serious violent behavior by individual chronic offenders (Papachristos, Meares, & Fagan, 2007). Focused deterrence has been applied to a wider range of problems, such as intimate partner violence (Kennedy, 2004, 2012; Sechrist & Weil, 2014), serious violence in maximum security prisons

(Warner, 2014), and covert opioid markets (Kennedy, 2016), with some very promising crime reduction impacts (National Network for Safe Communities, 2015, 2016; MacQuarrie, 2015). However, relative to the three core strategies, there is much less practical experience and empirical evidence to consider in these other applications.

Given the strong evaluation evidence showing crime reduction benefits and promising results indicating improved police-community relations, it is not surprising that focused deterrence has become a very popular way to address recurring crime problems. The U.S. Department of Justice has promoted its use through federally sponsored violence prevention programs such as the Strategic Approaches to Community Safety Initiative and Project Safe Neighborhoods (PSN) (Dalton, 2002). The National Network for Safe Communities (NNSC), an organization that supports the adoption of focused deterrence strategies, reports that it is currently active with some 42 cities across the United States. Experiences in Glasgow, Scotland; Malmo, Sweden; and Pelotas, Brazil suggest that the approach may be beneficial in addressing serious violence problems in other western countries (Deuchar, 2013; The Local, 2019; Borges, Rojido, & Cano, 2019). Police executives and other public officials in Middle Eastern and South American countries, such as Turkey, Israel, and Brazil, have also explored the possibility of implementing focused deterrence strategies to control gang and group-related violence in their cities (NNSC, 2013).

This Element begins with a brief discussion of the key steps in focused deterrence operations and its basic principles. Readers will soon note that the term focused deterrence is somewhat of a misnomer. The approach could also be referred to as strategies of fairness and focus, given the attention the work pays to enhancing police legitimacy through its highly economical use of criminal justice resources, transparency, respectful treatment of offenders, provision of social services, and community engagement (Kennedy, Kleiman, & Braga, 2017). The Element then reviews the available program evaluation evidence showing robust crime prevention impacts. The broader theoretical perspectives supporting the crime control efficacy of the approach – optimizing deterrence, promoting legitimacy and procedural justice, mobilizing informal social control, and reducing opportunities through situational crime prevention – are then considered. Avoiding well-known implementation obstacles by creating networks of capacity, developing accountability structures and sustainability plans, and conducting upfront and ongoing problem analysis is discussed in the next to last section. The Element concludes with a summary of the key theoretical and practical contributions of the approach to fair and effective crime control and prevention.

1.1 What Is Focused Deterrence?

Focused deterrence strategies are often framed as problem-oriented exercises in which specific recurring crime problems are analyzed, and responses are highly customized to local conditions and operational capacities (Kennedy, 2008). These strategies seek to change offender behavior by understanding underlying violence-producing dynamics and conditions that sustain recurring violence problems, and implementing a blended set of law enforcement, informal social control, and social service actions. In practice, these are frequently enhanced by attention to a broad range of associated situational factors (Braga & Kennedy, 2012). As described by Kennedy (2006: 156–7), focused deterrence operations have tended to follow this basic framework:

- Selecting a particular crime problem, such as serious gun violence.
- Pulling together an interagency enforcement group, typically including police, probation, parole, state and federal prosecutors, and sometimes federal enforcement agencies.
- Conducting research, usually relying heavily on the field experience of front-line police officers, to identify key offenders – and frequently groups of offenders, such as street gangs, drug crews, and the like – and the context of their behavior.
- Framing a special enforcement operation directed at those offenders and groups of offenders, and designed to substantially influence that context, for example by using any and all legal tools (or levers) to sanction groups such as drug-selling crews whose members commit serious violence.
- Matching those enforcement operations with parallel efforts to direct services and the moral voices of affected communities to those same offenders and groups.
- Communicating directly and repeatedly with offenders and groups to let them know that they are under particular scrutiny, what acts (such as shootings) will get special attention, when that has in fact happened to particular offenders and groups, and what they can do to avoid enforcement action; to emphasize community norms; and to specify the availability of supportive services.

This list provides a clear sense for the steps involved in a particular focused deterrence operation. For instance, putting together a working group of representatives from relevant criminal justice, social service, and community-based organizations who can bring varied incentives and disincentives to influence targeted offender behavior is a key early operational step.

However, the backbone of the basic philosophy and applied work of focused deterrence has emerged as a set of basic principles rather than a series of steps. Not all focused deterrence programs embrace each of these principles. Nevertheless, most programs go beyond either simple or unalloyed deterrence thinking and action. This set of principles is briefly described here.

1.1.1 Most Serious Crime Is Driven by a Small Number of Offenders

Serious crime concentrates among individuals, and a small number of chronic offenders generate a disparate share of the crime problem. In their classic study of nearly 10,000 boys in Philadelphia, Wolfgang, Figlio, and Sellin (1972) revealed that the most active 6 percent of delinquent boys were responsible for more than 50 percent of all delinquent acts committed. Laub and Sampson's (2003) close examination of a small set of persistent violent offenders revealed that these men were arrested on average 40 times over the course of their criminal career (the most active offender had been arrested 106 times) and spent an inordinate amount of time in prisons and jails. Over their full life course, these men were incarcerated on average seventy-five days each year. Similarly, the RAND Corporation's survey of jail and prison inmates in California, Michigan, and Texas revealed that, in all three states, the most recidivist 10 percent of active offenders committed some 50 percent of all crimes and 80 percent of crimes were committed by only 20 percent of the criminals (Chaiken & Chaiken, 1982). Moreover, the worst 1 percent of offenders committed crimes at an extremely high rate – more than fifty serious offenses per year (Rolph et al., 1981).

A recent systematic review of seventy-three studies examining the concentration of offending found that 10 percent of the most criminally active people from populations that included offenders and nonoffenders accounted for around 66 percent of crime (Martinez et al., 2017). The review also found that the most active 10 percent of offenders accounted for around 41 percent of crime committed by all offenders (Martinez et al., 2017). This skewed distribution is evident for many specific crime types. For example, overt community drug markets are typically driven by not more than a few score low-level dealers, and often much smaller numbers (Saunders et al., 2016); careful identification of the most dangerous domestic violence offenders in a town of just over 100,000 population found, at any given time, only about twenty (High Point Police Department, 2014); the core heroin supply and distribution network in a small American city was again only twenty or so dealers (NNSC, 2016). A recent review of research in more than twenty cities found that in the aggregate about 0.6 percent of the population was in groups associated with half of all gun violence (Lurie, 2019). A study of college students found that of 1882, 120 – about 6 percent – had committed rape. Seventy-six repeat rapists – 4 percent of the sample – averaged nearly six rapes apiece and collectively represented nearly 91 percent of all rapes (Lisak & Miller, 2002).

1.1.2 Chronicity, Range, and Victimization

Highly active violent offenders often commit a wide range of crimes (Spelman, 1990). For instance, the criminal careers of most Boston homicide offenders were characterized by a wide range of offense types including armed and unarmed violent offenses, illegal gun possession offenses, property offenses, drug offenses, and disorder offenses (Kennedy, Piehl, & Braga, 1996; Braga, Hureau, & Winship, 2008). The 120 rapists in Lisak and Miller's study admitted to 1,225 other violent acts, including "battery, physical abuse and/or sexual abuse of children, and sexual assault short of rape or attempted rape"; the 76 repeat rapists accounted for 85 percent of these acts (Lisak & Miller, 2002). Langford et al. (2000: 55) examined intimate partner homicide offenders in Massachusetts and found that 74 percent had a previous criminal record; 71 percent of those had records including previous violent offenses.

More generally, there is a robust literature on the wide range of offending and other risky behaviors amongst chronic and serious violent offenders. Research has consistently suggested a strong association between subcultural norms, exposure to neighborhood violence, and participation in offending and experiencing victimization (Jennings, Piquero, & Reingle, 2012). Studies have found the concentration and co-occurrence of violent offending, violent victimization, other crimes, drug and alcohol use, traffic offenses, and the like (Turanovic, Reisig, & Pratt, 2015; Osgood et al., 1988). The gang literature finds such "cafeteria style offending" a central aspect of gangs and gang dynamics (Klein, 1995). The Boston Gun Project examined victims and offenders associated with 155 youth gun and knife fatalities (Kennedy, Braga, & Piehl, 2001: 20):

> Prior to their murders, 75 percent of victims had been arraigned for at least one offense in Massachusetts courts, 19 percent had been committed to an adult or youth correctional facility, 42 percent had been on probation at some time before their murder, and 14 percent were on probation at the time of their murder. Of the 125 offenders known to be associated with those homicides, 77 percent had been arraigned for at least one offense in Massachusetts courts, 26 percent had been committed to a facility, 54 percent had been on probation, and 26 percent were on probation at the time they committed the murder. For the 117 homicide victims with at least one arraignment, the average number of arraignments was 9.5, and 44 percent had 10 or more arraignments. For the 96 offenders with at least one arraignment, the average number of arraignments was 9.7, and 41 percent had 10 or more arraignments. For both victims and offenders, arraignments for property offenses, armed violent offenses, and disorder offenses outnumbered drug offenses. For offenders, unarmed violent offenses also outnumbered drug offenses. Even within this high-rate population, offending was skewed, with the worst 5 percent and worst 10 percent of the 125 offenders responsible for 20 percent

and 36 percent of 1,009 total arraignments, respectively. The worst 5 percent and worst 10 percent of the 155 victims were responsible for 17 percent and 33 percent of 1,277 total arraignments, respectively.

While this is a perspective usually associated with a focus on offenders and offending, it is frequently associated with, and in certain circumstances is most usefully understood as driven by, extremely high levels of victimization, risk, and trauma. It was not as easy to examine victimization in the Boston research as it was offending, but a simple calculation of gang member mortality versus the Boston gang population showed roughly a one-in-seven chance of dying, almost entirely by gunshot, over a hypothetical ten-year gang membership spell (Kennedy, Piehl, & Braga, 1996). The gang literature is replete with findings that gang membership is driven by a desire for self-protection and objective risk from other gangs, and that gang members do not like gangs and the gang life and are under unwelcome pressure from both their enemies and their friends (Vigil, 1988; Padilla, 1992; Pitts, 2007). The "risky behavior" literature describes a milieu saturated in drug and alcohol abuse, intimate partner and sexual victimization, other assaults, disease and illness, traffic and other accidents, and repeated contact with police and the criminal justice system, with inevitable associated trauma (see, e.g., Donovan & Jessor, 1985; Leigh, 1999; Collins, Snodgrass, & Wheeless, 1999). Operational or research exposure to these issues reveals an "offending" population that is overwhelmingly poor; desperate; afraid; saturated in direct and vicarious violent victimization, both at home and in the community; frequently nearly or actually homeless; afraid for their friends and families; and afraid of the police and other authorities. Despite the common legal and popular separation of offender and offending, and victim and victimization, in practice they are very frequently essentially inseparable.

1.1.3 The Salience of Group and Collective Dynamics

When considering the problem of repeat offenders, an important dimension to consider is co-offending, or the commission of crimes by groups of offenders. In his analyses of victimization data in the United States for 2000 through 2005, Cook (2009) notes that nearly half of all robberies were committed by groups of offenders and the chances of a successful robbery directly correlated with the presence of accomplices. Youth, in particular, commit crimes, as they live their lives, in groups (Zimring, 1981). This observation is particularly important because youth offenders account for a disproportionate share of the most serious crimes. In his review of juvenile self-report survey data studies, Warr (2002) reports that most studies find between 50 and 75 percent of juvenile crimes are committed in the company of others. Youth gun violence is usually concentrated among groups of serious offenders, and conflicts between youth street gangs have long been noted to fuel much of the serious street violence in major cities (Miller, 1975; Braga, 2004; Howell & Griffiths, 2016). City-level studies have found gang-related motives in more than one-third of homicides in Chicago (Block & Block, 1993), 50 percent of the homicides in Los Angeles' Boyle Heights area (Tita et al., 2004), and 75 percent of homicides in Lowell, Massachusetts (Braga et al., 2006).

Recent research has further shown that the greatest concentration of gun homicide and nonfatal shooting occurs among individuals who are usually well-known to the criminal justice system (Cook, Ludwig, & Braga, 2005) and often involved in gangs and other high-risk co-offending networks (Papachristos, Braga, & Hureau, 2012). The rates of nonfatal and fatal shootings *within* such co-offending networks are considerably higher than both city-level rates as well as the rates within high-crime communities in those cities. In Chicago, for example, one study found that 70 percent of all fatal and nonfatal gunshot injuries occurred in identifiable networks composed of individuals arrested in previous years that comprised less than 6 percent of the city's total population; the rate of gun homicide in the network was more than nine times higher than the city as a whole (Papachristos, Wildeman, & Roberto, 2015). Much of the violence driven by high-risk gangs and criminally active groups in these networks is expressive in nature and often involves ongoing cycles of retaliation (Decker, 1996).

Such collective dynamics fundamentally change the nature of violent offending and victimization, and our understanding of what drives it. A long-standing vendetta between two groups, for example, is less about the individuals in the groups at any given time than it is about the collective transmittal of and adherence to norms and narratives around brotherhood, respect, risk, and desert. A criminal justice response that, for example, "clears" each of the last two shootings by incapacitating the last shooter from each group will have little or no impact on subsequent violence, which inheres in the groups as such and their standing conflict. It is even possible for all individuals involved in such dynamics to individually reject them while committing to sustained violent offending, for example through the "pluralistic ignorance" by which individuals adhere to perceived, but inaccurate, group norms (Matza, 1964)

1.1.4 Creating Certainty and Swiftness

Focused deterrence programs attempt to create a more certain and swift sanction environment through the creative application of existing enforcement capacity and legal authority (Kennedy, Kleiman, & Braga, 2017). The approach does so by separating the application of legal sanctions from the formal case processing activities of the criminal justice system, and separating the larger notion of deterrence from a reliance on the criminal justice system alone. The first separation involves discretionary application of existing legal authority in ways not formally connected to the underlying act. A person known to have committed a homicide, when that homicide cannot be prosecuted, can be subjected to legal attention for, for example, drug trafficking, a separate assault, receiving stolen property, and so on. Each member of a violent group not legally open to a collective legal response under conspiracy statutes can be subjected to individualized drug dealing or other charges. Such actions are of course not unheard of in criminal justice: the famously violent American gangster Al Capone was imprisoned by federal authorities on tax evasion charges. Focused deterrence had given that old insight theoretical foundation and practical systematization.

The second separation involves bringing to bear consequences entirely outside the criminal justice system. A violent offender living in rental housing can be evicted by their landlord under the provisions of the civil law. A drug group operating in the public street can be disrupted by redirecting traffic flow; if they are separated from customers, they will lose money. In Philadelphia, authorities discovered that gang members frequently lived in homes where they were stealing electric power and cable television services through illegal "pirate" connections; in the wake of violence, authorities mobilized providers to remove the illegal connections (Roman, Forney, et al., 2019). Even more than the creative use of legal authority, the use of such other measures serves to return deterrence to its fundamental insight that actions that come with costs will tend to be carried out less frequently.

This forms the basis of the "pulling levers" exercise within the focused deterrence framework. The traditional criminal justice response to a gang homicide is typically neither swift nor certain as action can be extraordinarily difficult and sometimes not possible (Wellford & Cronin, 1999; Braga, Turchan, & Barao, 2019). Authorities often know what happened but can't assemble the evidence and witnesses required to produce arrests and convictions. They may also know what happened in a way that cannot even in principle support legal action: that, for example, a particular gang is responsible for a homicide, without knowing what particular gang member. However, when the focus is on responding to the most violent gang in a particular jurisdiction, authorities can act through means such as warrant service, review and follow-up on open investigations, drug market disruption, civil code and traffic enforcement, closely monitoring and perhaps enhancing probation and parole conditions, more vigilant prosecutorial attention to existing legal liabilities, revisiting old offenses for new investigations, and so forth. In one instance involving a group of violent juveniles – who because of their status were open to essentially no legal sanctions – authorities disrupted the area of a public park they had established as their turf by trimming trees and shrubs and installing lighting to expose their activities to public view, cut off the public power outlets they were using to power their phones and video games, and had a local business password-protect the wireless router they had been using to upload provocative social media. Deterrence is produced when the targeted group and other groups watching the operations unfold understand what triggered the response and that similar actions will produce similar enforcement operations in the future – essentially, drawing "cause and effect" in the minds of offenders and prospective offenders alike (Kennedy, 1997, 2008).

Careful collection and analysis of intelligence and crime data provides the interagency working group with a clear understanding of who is doing what and aids the process of communicating appropriately focused sanction prospects. There are obvious and important due process, accountability, and justice concerns in launching such as strategy (Stuntz, 2011). However, the partnership structure, visibility, and transparency included in focused deterrence strategies can be protective assets that can manage these concerns (Thacher, 2016). It is also important to note that focused deterrence deliberately sacrifices the severity of sanctions in preference for the swift and certain application of sanctions. Economizing on punishment reduces harm to the offender. The working group charged with implementing the strategy searches for the "minimum effective dose" of a sanction that is needed to create compliance (Kennedy, Kleiman, & Braga, 2017). In theory and practice, group-focused deterrence is based on the premise that it is not the severity of individual sanctions that produces violence reductions, but the knowledge on the part of group members that violence will produce some, often relatively low-level, cost to a critical mass of group members, which then drives changes in group dynamics.

1.1.5 Launching Effective Communications

Deterrence essentially strives to reduce crime by changing potential offenders' *perceptions* of official action and associated risk of sanctions (Cook, 1980; Nagin, 2013). As such, an effective deterrence schema necessarily involves both *advertising* and *persuasion* (Zimring & Hawkins, 1973). Potential offenders need to know the punishment risks they face and need to believe that these risks are real. While this is theoretically obvious, deliberate communication with potential offenders has been neglected in practice (Kennedy, 2008). Focused deterrence places a premium on effective communication with potential offenders to produce crime control and prevention impacts.

Communicating credible warnings about enforcement actions serves two important goals. First, effective messages reduce the amount of sanction needed to change offender behavior. Second, warnings create legitimacy by supporting the perception that sanctions, when needed, will be applied in a fair manner after appropriate notice to targeted persons. Research shows clearly that offenders and potential offenders frequently do not know their legal risks (Kleck et al., 2005). There is no way they can know their legal risks when, for example, the law changes without publicity, or authorities make a discretionary decision to change their enforcement practices and priorities. In each case, what is not known cannot deter and the application of authority may be regarded as illegitimate and unfair.

Communication sessions with offenders can be used to convey not only enforcement risks but also "moral voice" and "outreach and support" messages. These encounters can model procedural justice and legitimacy, and foster new perceptions and relationships about and between criminal justice agencies, community members, and potential offenders (Papachristos, Meares, & Fagan, 2007; Trinkner, 2019). Two key communication mechanisms tend to be used in focused deterrence programs (Kennedy & Friedrich, 2014). *Call-ins* are carefully staged events that bring the operational partners into contact with groups of potential offenders at a set time in a predetermined location. They generally involve from twenty to forty group members (or in the case of individual-focused intervention, high-risk or repeat potential offenders; law enforcement officials, community members, and service providers; and some-time other participants and observers. In the classic GVI call-in, the purpose is to identify group members and to use the call-in to convey key messages through them back to their groups: the call-in is largely about the larger universe of groups and group members, and less about those group members actually present. *Custom notifications* involve more immediate, pressing, and discretionary communications to high-risk individuals who are likely to commit violence in the near term. Authorities seek out such risky people and convey core messages to them in person: the potentially violent situation is known and being monitored, the community disapproves of such violence, violence will bring unwanted consequences, and help is available.

1.1.6 Providing Outreach and Support

Focused deterrence programs provide outreach and support – social services and various kinds of facilitative interventions – to the identified high-risk populations. The role of outreach and support in focused deterrence is complex (Kennedy, Kleiman, & Braga, 2017). There is hope that support services can reduce individual offending. However, even if services do not generate the desired crime prevention impacts, the offering of these opportunities may change offending dynamics by making it more difficult for offenders to justify their ongoing criminal behavior (known as "removing excuses" in situational crime prevention; Clarke, 1997). Service portfolios originally comprised mostly traditional offerings such as job training and placement, education and remedial education, life skills, substance abuse treatment, mental health services, and the like. Unfortunately, the actual outcomes of these traditional social service and opportunity provision strategies in the focused deterrence framework have not been encouraging. In most cities that implemented GVI, very few targeted offenders actually took advantage of such traditional services, and the outcomes associated with such services have been generally poor (NNSC, 2014). In Cincinnati, an evaluation found no association between violence reduction outcomes and the number of people who received services through the CIRV program (Engel, Tillyer & Corsaro 2013).

Anecdotal evidence suggests that the provision of social services and various types of facilitative interventions to identified high-risk populations through outreach and support efforts seems to be an important step toward improving the perceived legitimacy and procedural fairness of the focused deterrence approach (Kennedy, 2011). Nevertheless, the apparent failure of the social service outreach work has led to the development of a broader portfolio of offerings that may be more relevant to the immediate needs of this very high-risk population: immediate protection from harm, including intervention with enemies and temporary and permanent relocation; the acquisition of drivers' licenses and other identification documents; food, clothing, and shelter; a recognition of the trauma associated with exposure to high levels of violence and high levels of criminal justice system contact; assistance with issues associated with criminal justice system contact, such as outstanding warrants, fines, child support judgments, and criminal records; and the facilitation of relationships with mainstream individuals and institutions (NNSC, 2014). This new menu has led to enhanced participation and uptake; however, any effects on individual outcomes, crime outcomes, and legitimacy have not yet been determined through rigorous program evaluation.

1.1.7 Promoting Legitimacy and Procedural Justice

Research suggests positive community perceptions of the legitimacy of criminal justice institutions are associated with lower levels of violence (Kirk & Papachristos, 2011), and authorities need public support and cooperation to be effective in controlling crime (Tyler, 2006; Bottoms & Tankebe, 2012). How citizens experience their interactions with the police and other legal authorities influences their sense of procedural justice in these encounters, which in turn impacts their perceptions of legitimacy and willingness to comply with the law, comply with directives, and cooperate with requests for help (Tyler, 2006). Unfortunately, weak relationships between the police and residents of disadvantaged communities of color undermine effective crime prevention and crime prevention strategies in many urban environments.

Poor police–minority community relationships are rooted in a long history of discriminatory practices and contemporary proactive policing strategies that are overly aggressive and associated with racial disparities (Braga, Brunson, & Drakulich, 2019). Despite widespread belief to the contrary, high-crime communities have very low tolerance for violence and disorder and have a high degree of respect for the law and law-abidingness (Sampson & Bartusch, 1998). The same is true for even many serious violent offenders (Papachristos, Meares, & Fagan, 2012). Both, however, have low respect for and confidence in the police. Research shows that proximate community and individual experiences that reduce legitimacy are associated with decreased cooperation with police and higher levels of violent crime (Kirk & Papachristos, 2011), higher rates of gun acquisition and carrying (Sierra-Arévalo, 2016), and higher rates of criminality (Tyler, Fagan, & Geller, 2014). Focused deterrence programs attempt to promote legitimacy by ensuring that crime control efforts are focused on the safety and well-being (including preventing their involvement in the criminal justice system) of group members and others at high risk; not indiscriminate and unfocused; that triggering events and subsequent enforcement actions are transparent to community members and offenders alike; that community members are engaged in the design and implementation of the intervention; that contacts between potential offenders and the authorities are procedurally just; and that offers of help and assistance are serious and meaningful (Kennedy, 2011).

Legitimacy and procedural justice in focused deterrence has been most explicitly brought to bear on the settings in which authorities directly communicate with potential offenders and the framing and content of those communications (Wallace et al., 2016). The content of these messages and their intended impacts on offender behaviors are described in much greater detail later in this Element. Most recently, the framework of procedural justice and legitimacy has expanded to include attention to racialized conflict between communities and law enforcement, and to reconciliation processes as responses to those conflicts (Kennedy & Ben-Menachem, 2019; Mentel, 2012; Meares, 2009). In essence, the community reconciliation efforts attempt to find common ground between legal authorities and community members through frank conversations that recognize the role of police and the law in the historical and present oppression of communities, create opportunities for community members to speak to experiences and narratives, and create links to repair harm and change official policies and practices. These engagements are intended to mobilize community informal social control, enhance voluntary compliance with the law, and build working relationships between communities and police. They have been central elements of initiatives with impacts that have been confirmed by rigorous evaluations, but have not been evaluated independently (Saunders et al., 2015; La Vigne et al., 2019)

After the focused deterrence implementation is launched, the partnership must follow up relentlessly to ensure that any promises that were made are kept (Kennedy, 2011; Abt, 2019). This is particularly salient after messages are communicated to prospective offenders. Effectiveness will be undermined if offenders break the rules set by the working group and no sanctions are delivered, and if they ask for support and do not get it. Any gains in legitimacy made as a result of procedurally just discussions during call-ins will be diminished if protection, services, opportunities, and other resources are not provided. In essence, criminal justice, social service, and community-based partners should never "write a check that can't be cashed." More generally, partnering agencies should also keep any promises made at the outset of the process on the resources required to ensure a robust implementation. Delivering on these broader promises helps to keep partners united and focused on the crime prevention task at hand. Assessment and evaluation help to ensure promises are kept.

1.1.8 Assessing and Evaluating

Consistent with its problem-oriented policing origins, an important part of focused deterrence practice involves assessing the impact the intervention had on the crime problem it intended to address (Goldstein, 1990; Braga, 2008a). It is worth distinguishing between assessment and evaluation here. Evaluation is a scientific process for establishing whether an intervention (such as focused deterrence) caused an observable impact on an outcome (such as gun homicides). An *impact evaluation* focuses on questions of crime prevention effectiveness (e.g., did the problem decline? If so, did the implemented response cause the decline?), while a *process evaluation* focuses on questions of accountability and integrity in response implementation (e.g., did the response occur as planned? Did all the response components work?). Jurisdictions implementing focused deterrence should conduct both. Assessment is the culmination of the evaluation process and represents the final stage where it is determined whether the targeted problem changed as a result of the implemented response and decisions are made about continuing the response, trying alternative responses, and applying an "effective" response to other places, people, and situations (Eck, 2002).

There are at least three critical reasons to conduct an assessment. First, assessment ensures that the partnering agencies remain accountable for their performance and for their use of resources. It is important to track the various activities of interagency working groups to make certain the strategy is being implemented with high integrity. Second, assessment allows the partnering agencies to learn about what focused deterrence methods are effective in dealing with selected problems in their specific operational environment. Unless someone checks to see whether their efforts produced the desired outcome, it will be difficult for partnering agencies to improve their practices. Third, assessment makes it possible to determine when an intervention is not working so partnering agencies can figure out why and adjust the response in ways to make it more effective. There are many reasons why a targeted crime problem might not by impacted by an implemented intervention. For instance, the targeted problem may not have been analyzed adequately and the implemented response might not fit the actual underlying conditions that cause a problem to persist. Whatever the reason, assessment identifies the performance gap and challenges practitioners to revisit the focused deterrence implementation.

2 The Emergence of Focused Deterrence

Police crime control efforts have evolved considerably over the last forty years. Faced with growing concerns over their effectiveness and efficiency, police agencies developed a wide range of innovative strategies that took a more active approach to controlling crime problems (Weisburd & Braga, 2019). These new crime control strategies included community-based interventions, problem-solving interventions, place-based interventions, and person-focused interventions (Weisburd & Majmundar, 2018). Some of these proactive policing programs involved intensive enforcement actions that some citizens regarded as controversial, leading to questions over whether these programs were implemented in a fair and unbiased manner (Tyler, Goff, & MacCoun, 2015; Eberhardt, 2019). These concerns were particularly salient for residents of disadvantaged minority neighborhoods who desperately needed effective policing to address serious crime and disorder problems but held longstanding concerns over how police services were being delivered in their communities (Braga, Brunson, & Drakulich, 2019). The focused deterrence approach developed and matured during this period of police innovation and intense debate over fairness and effectiveness in policing communities.

Focused deterrence is consistent with the observation that innovative policing programs that increase the focus of police prevention activities and expand the tools available to police officers are more effective in controlling crime and disorder (Weisburd & Eck, 2004). As will be described, the focused deterrence approach developed from a problem-oriented policing project to control serious youth violence in Boston during the 1990s (Kennedy, Piehl, & Braga, 1996). Problem-oriented policing generally seeks to analyze the under-lying conditions of a specific recurring crime problem, develop a customized response to those conditions that often includes alternative crime prevention actions, and evaluate whether the implemented response generated the desired impact on the targeted crime problem (Goldstein, 1990). While there are distinct programmatic elements and operational framework, focused deterrence strat-egies are often framed as problem-oriented exercises where targeted crime problems are analyzed, and responses are highly tailored to local conditions and operational capacities.

The next section describes the development and implementation of the Operation Ceasefire GVI in Boston during the 1990s. Subsequent sections describe the application of focused deterrence to disorderly street drug markets in High Point, North Carolina, and high-risk offenders in Chicago. Boston Ceasefire received national acclaim as a promising violence prevention strategy after youth homicides decreased by nearly two-thirds following its implementation. Unfortunately, the Ceasefire strategy was discontinued in 2000 and, by the mid-2000s, youth homicides and shootings reemerged as a citywide crisis. In 2007, Boston implemented a revitalized Ceasefire focused deterrence strategy after a problem analysis revealed that, once again, gang violence was driving citywide youth homicides. Serious gun violence immediately decreased following the Ceasefire GVI launch and Boston youth homicides have remained low through 2018.

2.1 The Development of the GVI: The Boston Gun Project and Operation Ceasefire

Many American cities experienced a sudden and large increase in gun violence soon after the crack cocaine epidemic emerged during the late 1980s and early 1990s (Blumstein, 1995). In Boston, the crack epidemic started in early 1986 and, soon after, Boston youth gangs became engaged in the crack trade, which led to increased acquisition of firearms (Kennedy, Piehl, & Braga, 1996; Braga, 2003). As Figure 1 reveals, Boston experienced about 28 homicides of youth 24 and younger per year between 1980 and 1988. Youth homicides then suddenly increased to a 1990 peak of 73 victims. The yearly number of Boston youth

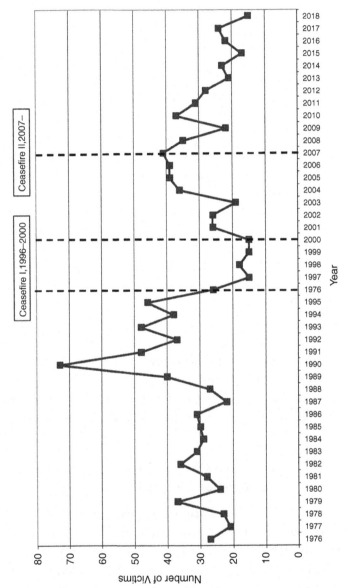

Figure 1. Youth Homicides in Boston, 1976–2018.

Source: Authors

homicides decreased after that peak but did not return to pre-crack epidemic levels and remained historically high. Boston averaged roughly 45 youth homicide victims per year between 1991 and 1995.

The Boston Police Department (BPD) and Harvard University researchers collaborated on a U.S. Department of Justice-sponsored problem-oriented policing enterprise, known as the Boston Gun Project, to develop an innovative response to the city's persistent youth homicide problem (Kennedy, Piehl & Braga, 1996). The Project was led by an interagency working group consisting of criminal justice, social service, and community-based partners. Harvard researchers completed a problem analysis that revealed the bulk of youth homicide was generated by a very small number of youths who were involved in ongoing gang violence. Youth homicide offenders and youth homicide victims were well known to the criminal justice system., involved in a variety of different crimes, and often on probation or under some other kind of criminal justice system control. Most youth homicides and shootings were highly concentrated in the disadvantaged and mostly minority neighborhoods of Roxbury, Dorchester, and Mattapan. The research showed that gun violence had become "decoupled" from the crack trade. It remained highly concentrated amongst members of drug crews, but was associated strongly with running group and individual vendettas, or "beefs"; group and individual retaliation; disputes over respect; issues around romantic partners; and the like.

The working group considered the problem analysis research findings in light of policy insights on effective applications of deterrence theory to reduce criminal offending and their past experiences using alternative approaches to quell outbreaks of gang violence (Kennedy, Braga, & Piehl, 2001). This process led to the development and implementation of the Operation Ceasefire focused deterrence strategy in May 1996. Consistent with the GVI elements described previously, Ceasefire involved direct communications to gangs through group call-ins and customized street conversations that homicides would not be tolerated, law enforcement operations tailored to repeat offending behaviors and criminal justice vulnerabilities of targeted gangs, powerful expressions of anti-violence community norms, and offers of social services and employment opportunities to gang members who wanted to change their life trajectories. The Ceasefire strategy was supported by a strong "network of capacity" of criminal justice, social service, and community-based organizations that enabled the working group to launch a robust response to gang violence through coordinated and combined efforts that magnified their separate effects (Braga, Turchan, & Winship, 2019). This eventually included a partnership with the Ten Point Coalition, consisting of a group of activist black clergy, who helped strengthen the legitimacy of the Ceasefire strategy and enhanced the political support of Boston's minority communities by providing a desirable mechanism for transparency and accountability in its application (Winship & Berrien, 1999).

Immediately following the mid-1996 launch of the Ceasefire focused deterrence strategy, Boston youth homicides decreased dramatically (Figure 1). As will be discussed further, a quasi-experimental evaluation found that Ceasefire was associated with a 63 percent reduction in youth homicide in Boston that was distinct from 1990s youth homicide trends in most large U.S. and New England cities (Braga et al., 2001). Partly due to the involvement of black ministers in the strategy, these surprising large reductions in youth homicide were called "The Boston Miracle" by the national media. The Ceasefire strategy was subsequently recognized with a series of prestigious awards including the Ford Foundation's Innovations in American Government Award (1997), the Police Executive Research Forum's Herman Goldstein Award recognizing excellence in problem-oriented policing (1998), and the International Association of Chiefs of Police's Webber Seavey Award recognizing quality in law enforcement (1999).

After several years of sustained reductions in youth homicides, the BPD halted the Ceasefire intervention in January 2000 (Braga, Turchan, & Winship, 2019). At that time, the BPD implemented a wider set of violence reduction programs including a reentry initiative to assist violent offenders to transition from jail back to their communities, a strategy to coordinate service delivery to high-risk families that generated and experienced repeat serious violence across generations, and an effort to improve unsolved shooting investigations. Regrettably, the broader slate of programs seemed to diffuse the capacity of the BPD and their partners to halt outbreaks of serious gang violence in Boston. Youth homicides soon started to increase. As Figure 1 shows, the yearly number of youths killed in Boston steadily increased from 15 victims in 2000 to 41 victims in 2007. During this time period, the BPD did not engage in strategic analyses of its increasing youth homicide problem. Further, there was substantial internal dysfunction in both the BPD and the influential Ten Point Coalition during these years that precluded the implementation of strategic response (Braga, Turchan, and Winship, 2019).

A new BPD commissioner was appointed at the end of 2006 and, with the start of 2007, a revitalized Ceasefire focused deterrence strategy was launched (Braga, Hureau, & Papachristos, 2014). A newly completed problem analysis revealed, once again, that Boston's youth homicide problem was largely driven by surging gang violence concentrated in the disadvantaged mostly minority Roxbury, Dorchester, and Mattapan neighborhoods of Boston (Braga, Hureau, & Winship, 2008). The yearly count of youth homicides with gang motives increased seven-fold between 1999 and 2006 – indeed, two-thirds of youth homicides had gang motives and 70 percent of nonfatal shootings involved gang members in 2006. The problem analysis further revealed that fatal and nonfatal shootings were largely carried out by 65 active street gangs representing roughly 1 percent of Boston's youth population between the ages of 15 and 24. One third of all shootings in 2006 were generated by only ten street gangs.

The Lucerne Street Doggz, a loosely organized street gang with roughly 50 members and active conflicts with eight rival gangs, was the first group selected for the post-2007 implementation of the Ceasefire GVI (Braga, Hureau, & Papachristos, 2014). The Doggz were involved in almost 10 percent of Boston's 377 total shootings in 2006 – they were suspected offenders in 30 shootings and victims in 7 shootings. Through the end of May 2007, the Lucerne Street Doggz were suspected of committing another 21 shootings and suffered an additional 6 shootings of its members. The reconstituted Ceasefire working group realized it was critical to mount a strong response to the persistent gun violence generated by the Doggz in order to reestablish the credibility of its anti-violence message to other street gangs.

The Ceasefire GVI resulted in a sudden large decrease in shootings by and against the Lucerne Street Doggz (Figure 2). Between 2006 and 2007, the Doggz averaged almost 34 total shootings per year. The yearly number of shootings involving the Doggz decreased by roughly 88 percent to a little more than four per year between 2008 and 2010. The Ceasefire working group subsequently marketed the highly effective Lucerne Street operation to

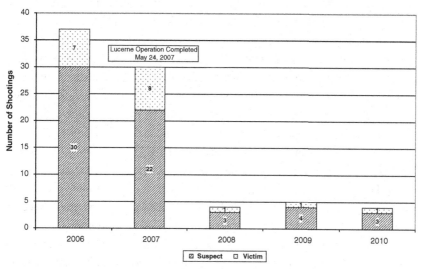

Figure 2. Total Shootings Involving Lucerne Street Doggz, 2006 – 2010.
Source: Braga, Hureau, & Papachristos (2014: 133).

other Boston street gangs as credible evidence that outbreaks of gun violence would be met with a swift and certain law enforcement response. Between 2007 and 2010, the Ceasefire working group engaged with 19 Boston gangs through the reconstituted GVI. A quasi-experimental evaluation of the post-2007 Ceasefire GVI found that total shootings involving treated Boston gangs decreased by 31 percent relative to total shootings involving matched comparison Boston gangs (Braga, Hureau, & Papachristos, 2014). Citywide youth homicides in Boston also decreased by almost two-thirds from 41 victims in 2007 to 15 victims in 2018 (Figure 1).

After the mid-1990s experience with Operation Ceasefire, numerous replications followed rapidly. Those interventions and their impact will be addressed in the next sections.

2.2 The Development of the DMI: Drug Market Intervention in High Point, North Carolina

After the surprising success of the Ceasefire DMI in Boston, the U.S. Department of Justice launched the Strategic Approaches to Community Safety Initiative (SACSI) in 1998. This initiative supported the implementation of the basic problem-solving framework pioneered in Boston to a broader range of crime problems in ten communities (Dalton, 2002). SACSI aided the implementation of several focused deterrence interventions in these communities, including GVI programs that were found to be effective in reducing gang violence in Indianapolis (McGarrell et al., 2006) and Rochester, New York (Roehl et al., 2008). In 2001, these promising experiences led the Bush Administration to establish Project Safe Neighborhoods (PSN) to support innovation in reducing gun violence in all 94 federal judicial districts, an initiative that continues at the time of writing. In each district, U.S. Attorney's Offices coordinated partnerships between local-state-federal law enforcement organizations, other criminal justice agencies, and community-based groups that were required to implement research-based problem-solving strategies to blend prevention, intervention, and enforcement activities to address gun violence problems. A national evaluation of PSN found that these activities generated significant reductions in violent crime and gun homicides in districts that implemented the program with sufficient intensity and focus (McGarrell et al., 2010).

The DMI was developed in the context of this broader background of national interest in and experimentation with focused deterrence strategies. Several cities in the Middle District of North Carolina tested GVI programs to control gang-related gun violence during the late 1990s and early 2000s (Frabutt et al., 2009). High Point (NC) is a relatively small city covering roughly 50 square miles and, according to 2000 U.S. Census, populated by roughly 100,000 residents. The High Point Police Department (HPPD) experienced success with focused deterrence and, based on these positive experiences, a newly appointed police chief decided to apply the focused deterrence approach to deal with violence and disorder emanating from overt street-level drug markets in 2003 (Kennedy, 2009a).

The core logic of DMI was, like that of GVI, fairly simple. It held that the public safety problems associated with overt ("open air," which in practice could include houses, apartments, and the like) markets was associated with the violent and chaotic market, not drug dealing or use as such; that geographically defined overt markets had tremendous staying power, as both sellers and buyers knew that they could do business there and were repeatedly drawn to them, making them resistant to ordinary enforcement and prevention approaches (a collective dynamic different than that found in group-related violence, but one that made the issue also importantly distinct from individual actors); and that the market could be permanently eliminated if it were disrupted long enough for both sellers and buyers to cease expecting they could do business there and no longer have any reason to return. In practice that disruption could be produced by stopping the small number of dealers at the lowest level of the market for long enough to break the cycle, and then preventing any dealer from beginning to reestablish the market (Kennedy, 2009a).

It proved impossible to get either police departments or communities to engage in the logic of such an approach. Such consideration was blocked by deeply grooved and mutually destructive narratives held on both sides. Police believed the affected communities supported the dealing and were living off drug money; communities believed the police could stop the dealing if they wanted to and were complicit or instrumental in the drug trade in order to harm the neighborhood and its residents (Kennedy, 2011). In High Point, the DMI was informed by an explicit recognition of this dynamic and the framing of a deliberate police/community reconciliation process. This engagement, led by the HPPD chief, was brutally honest about the harms and failures imposed on disadvantaged black communities by past policing regimes and attempted to reconcile with residents by promising carefully constructed community crime prevention strategies designed to reduce arrests, particularly of young black men (Kennedy, 2009a). These frank conversations about race, drugs, and policing positioned the HPPD to partner with West End neighborhood residents to launch a focused deterrence strategy to address violence and disorder emanating from a highly active street drug market.

As described by Kennedy (2009a), the DMI proceeded by first conducting careful data analyses and intelligence gathering on key participants in the targeted drug market, which identified less than twenty dealers rather than the hundreds that police had assumed. Undercover drug buys were then made from all identified dealers in the West End drug market. Nonviolent dealers had their cases "banked" – suspended without action – rather than being arrested. This move both created a powerful deterrent – those dealers with banked cases could be told that any visible new dealing would lead to their immediate arrest and prosecution, as opposed to the rare and unpredictable risks they were accustomed to – and were a concrete demonstration to the community that police were not conspiring to arrest its young men. The nonviolent dealers were brought to a call-in where they faced a roomful of law enforcement officers, social service providers, community figures, ex-offenders, and "influentials" – parents, relatives, and others with close, important relationships with particular dealers. Table 1 presents the key steps in the process.

During the call-in session, the nonviolent drug dealers were told that (1) they were valuable to the community, and (2) the dealing must stop (Kennedy, 2009a). Community members and influentials sent a norm-changing message to the participants by describing the harm that drug dealing was doing to the neighborhood and voiced support of their capacity to change these behaviors. Social services and opportunities were offered to the dealers. Ex-offenders explained how they successfully made the transition from drug selling to employment. Law enforcement officials then informed the dealers that they faced pending drug charges and showed videos of the undercover buys from each of the call-in participants (Kennedy & Wong, 2009). The officials told dealers that they were not being arrested; that neither police nor the community wanted them arrested; but that the cases would be activated if they continued to sell drugs. The West End

Table 1. Stages and Operational Steps for the Drug Market Intervention.

Stage	Operational Step
Identification	Identifying the Target Area through Crime Mapping
	Engaging the Community
	Engaging the Police Department Internally
	Identifying Street Drug Offenders
	Reviewing Street Drug Incidents to Refine the List
	Conducting the Undercover Operation
Notification	Establishing Contact with the Offender's Family
	Conducting the Notification
Resource Delivery and	Setting a Deadline
Community Support	Strict Enforcement
	Follow-up

Source: Adapted from Frabutt et al. (2009: 122)

call-in was supported by the continued delivery of resources and a "maintenance" strategy designed to identify and respond immediately to any new dealing, and thus prevent the reemergence of the market.

The High Point DMI was implemented on a rolling basis across neighborhoods suffering from overt drug market problems (Kennedy & Wong, 2009). In each site, data analyses and investigation of key drug market offenders lasted between one and three months. These upfront activities ensured that enforcement was limited to very modest numbers of individuals directly involved in the street drug trade. For instance, four call-in meetings were held with offenders from four different neighborhoods between 2004 and 2007 (Kennedy & Wong, 2009). As described previously, key offenders with prior violent felony convictions were arrested while nonviolent offenders were selected to participate in the call-ins. In total, 83 dealers were identified across the four intervention locations; 20 were arrested and 63 were selected to participate in a call-in (Corsaro et al., 2012). At all call-ins, the message communicated to participants consisted of deterrence, social services and opportunity, and changing norms.

A series of evaluations found that the High Point DMI produced significant reductions in crime. In a descriptive assessment of the West End intervention, Kennedy and Wong (2009) reported that the target drug market disappeared in the treatment area (as measured by direct observation and mechanisms such as attempted drug buys by undercover officers and informants) and that violent crime decreased 39 percent and drug crime decreased by 30 percent. In a more rigorous quasi-experimental evaluation, Corsaro et al. (2012) analyzed longitudinal data to estimate program effects on violent crime trends in four treated High Point neighborhoods relative to violent crime trends in matched comparison High Point neighborhoods. This evaluation reported more modest 12- to 18-percent reductions in violent crime in the treated areas relative to control areas (Corsaro et al., 2012). Using a different methodology and a fifth treated neighborhood, RAND Corporation researchers applied a synthetic control group quasi-experimental design to evaluate the High Point DMI program and reported a 21 percent reduction in general crime rates in treated areas with little evidence of spatial crime displacement (Saunders et al., 2015).

Other assessments of the High Point DMI suggested improved perceptions of crime among residents (Frabutt et al., 2009) and decreased availability of drugs as indicated by more challenges when narcotic officers attempted to conduct undercover drug buys (Kennedy & Wong, 2009). Equally important, the truth and reconciliation efforts that accompanied the DMI implementation seemed to improve the willingness of black residents to collaborate with the HPPD on crime prevention strategies. Qualitative interviews with residents in the DMI drug market areas suggest police-community relations were greatly improved by the effectiveness of the focused deterrence strategy, coupled with the common ground generated by the police-led engagement efforts that acknowledged the past harms inflicted on the black community by the ineffective and inappropriate policing practices of the past (Frabutt et al., 2009). In 2007, the High Point DMI received the Ford Foundation's Innovations in American Government Award. In that same year, the promising evaluation findings led the U.S. Bureau of Justice Assistance to launch its DMI training and technical assistance program that provided more than 25 communities with guidance in developing and launching similar strategies. The lessons learned from these DMI replication efforts are described later.

2.3 The Development of the Individual Strategies: Project Safe Neighborhoods in Chicago

The Chicago PSN taskforce started meeting on a monthly basis in May 2002 to design gun violence reduction strategies in two adjacent Chicago Police Department (CPD) districts suffering from very high levels of serious gun violence (Papachristos, Meares, & Fagan, 2007). The PSN taskforce included representatives from the U.S. Attorney's Office for the Northern District of Illinois, CPD, Illinois Department of Correction, Cook County Department of Probation, Cook County State's Attorney's Office, City of Chicago Corporation Counsel, and more than a dozen community-based organizations. While multiple PSN initiatives were launched, Papachristos, Meares, and Fagan (2007) identified four key components that were directly focused on reducing gun violence in the targeted policing districts in the near term: offender notification meetings, federal prosecutions, federal prison sentences, and multiagency gun recoveries. The offender notification meetings represented the major community intervention, and the other components reflected coordinated law enforcement actions. Taken together, these components represent the basic elements of a focused deterrence strategy designed to change the behavior of high-risk individual offenders.

Offender notification meetings represent the key activity launched by the PSN taskforce to change the normative perceptions of gun violence held by the targeted population of high-risk offenders (Papachristos, Meares, & Fagan, 2007). Beginning in January 2003, the PSN taskforce held offender notification meetings twice per month with randomly selected offenders from the two treatment districts who had prior gun violence records and were recently assigned to probation or parole. The one-hour notification meetings stressed the consequences that offenders faced if they continued to use guns and the choices they needed to make to prevent further re-offending. Three distinct segments of the meeting reinforced this message: (1) law enforcement officials emphasized their enhanced efforts to reduce gun violence in the targeted communities and informed offenders of their exposure as felons to federal firearms laws with stiff mandatory minimum sentences, (2) ex-offenders from the community who work with social intervention programs described how they managed to turn away from violence and change their life trajectories, and (3) a series of speakers from community-based groups discussed the choices the offender could make to enroll or participate in specific social service and opportunity provision programs. These programs included substance-abuse assistance, temporary shelter, job training, mentorship and union training, education and GED courses, and behavior counseling.

Federal prosecutions of gun offenders and increased law enforcement efforts to recover illegal guns represented the on-the-ground enhanced risks of apprehension faced by former offenders being released under community supervision to the target areas (Papachristos, Meares, & Fagan, 2007). Multiagency PSN gun teams staffed by federal, county, and local law enforcement representatives concentrated their resources on gun crime in the two treatment districts. The gun teams investigated illegal gun sales and use, conducted gun seizures, and served warrants on pending firearm cases. On a biweekly basis, the broader PSN taskforce reviewed every gun case generated by the gun teams to determine whether a federal or state prosecution would lead to the longest prison sentences.

A quasi-experimental design was used to evaluate the impact of the various PSN programs on neighborhood-level homicide rates in Chicago (Papachristos, Meares, & Fagan, 2007). The two adjacent PSN police districts were statistically matched to two other police districts selected as near-equivalent controls. The research team analyzed the overall effects of the PSN treatment as well as the four interventions that comprised the PSN treatment: (1) increased federal prosecutions for convicted felons carrying or using guns, (2) the length of sentences associated with federal prosecutions, (3) gun recoveries by the gun teams, and (4) social marketing of deterrence and social norms messages through offender notification meetings. The research team found that the PSN treatment was associated with a statistically significant 37 percent reduction in the number of homicides in the treatment district relative to the control districts (see Figure 3). The overall PSN treatment was also associated with statistically significant decreases in gun homicide incidents and aggravated assault incidents, and a non-statistically significant decrease in gang homicide incidents.

The PSN component that generated the largest statistically significant effect on decreased homicide in the treatment districts relative to control districts was the offender notification forums. In short, the greater the proportion of offenders who attended the forums, the greater the decline in treatment district levels of

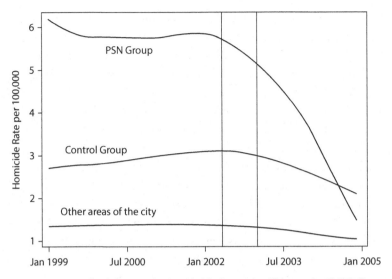

Figure 3. Smoothed Quarterly Homicide Rates in Chicago by PSN Group
Assignment, 1999–2004.

Source: Papachristos, Meares, & Fagan (2007: 256).

homicide. In a supplemental assessment, Wallace et al. (2016) focused on the offending behaviors of individuals after they attended a PSN offender notification meeting. Analyses suggested that notification meeting participants had 30 percent lower risk for committing new offenses when compared to similar offenders in no-treatment comparison groups. Papachristos, Meares, and Fagan (2007) also found that increased federal prosecutions and the number of guns recovered by the gun teams were associated with modest but statistically significant declines in homicides in the treatment districts relative to the control districts. Getting more guns off the street and prosecuting more offenders federally for gun crimes were associated with small but meaningful homicide decreases. The length of sentences associated with federal prosecutions was not associated with the observed homicide decreases.

The Chicago PSN strategy has been replicated in several places, to be discussed later.

3 The Empirical Evidence Supporting Focused Deterrence Crime Reduction Impacts

The surprising downturn in youth homicides in Boston associated with the Ceasefire focused deterrence strategy was greeted with a healthy dose of skepticism by practitioners and scholars alike. For instance, in his departing 2001 speech, former New York City Mayor Rudy Giuliani suggested that the

"Boston Model" did not lead to lasting violence reduction gains.[1] In *The New Yorker* magazine, Professor Franklin Zimring expressed concerns over the existing scientific evidence supporting focused deterrence programs at that time and suggested, "Ceasefire is more of a theory of treatment rather than a proven strategy" (Seabrook, 2009: 37). Even as practical experiences and rigorous evaluations increased and continued to support the crime control efficacy of the approach (see Braga & Weisburd, 2012), some scholars seemed to ignore the growing evidence base. For example, in 2013, former National Council on Crime and Delinquency president Barry Krisberg purported to summarize the available evidence by stating, "It certainly hasn't been effective so far, and there is no information suggesting it is effective."[2]

Other practitioners and scholars have been much more supportive of the empirical evidence supporting the crime reduction impacts of focused deterrence on targeted crime problems in Boston and elsewhere (e.g., Morgan & Winship, 2007; Cook & Ludwig, 2006). In his address to the American Society of Criminology, former U.S. National Institute of Justice Director Jeremy Travis (1998) recognized Boston's Operation Ceasefire as a promising violence reduction strategy and suggested that focused deterrence "has made enormous theoretical and practical contributions to our thinking about deterrence and the role of the criminal justice system in producing safety." More recently, the U.S. National Academies Committee on Proactive Policing (Weisburd & Majmundar, 2018: 310) concluded that "focused deterrence programs show consistent crime control impacts on gang violence, street crime driven by disorderly drug markets, and repeat individual offending." An ongoing systematic review of the program evaluation evidence has been highly influential in documenting the positive impacts of focused deterrence on crime (Braga & Weisburd, 2012; Braga, Weisburd, & Turchan, 2018).

3.1 Systematic Review of Focused Deterrence Programs

The most recent iteration of the systematic review identified twenty-four quasi-experimental evaluations of focused deterrence programs (Braga, Weisburd, & Turchan, 2018). Table 2 presents the basic features of the twenty-four included evaluations. These studies evaluated focused deterrence programs implemented in small, medium, and large cities. With the exception of an evaluation of a focused deterrence program implemented in Glasgow, Scotland, all included

---

[1] www.nytimes.com/2001/12/27/nyregion/text-of-mayor-giulianis-farewell-address.html (Accessed October 23, 2019).

[2] http://inthenews.berkeleylawblogs.org/2013/12/19/oakland-crime-strategy-has-failed-in-past/ (Accessed December 26, 2016).

Table 2. Characteristics of Focused Deterrence Evaluations in Systematic
Review. N=24

Characteristic	N	Percent
Country		
United States	23	95.8
Other (Scotland)	1	4.2
City Population		
Small (< 200,000 residents)	8	33.3
Medium (200,000 – 500,000 residents)	6	25.0
Large (> 500,000 residents)	10	41.7
Study Type		
Quasi-experiment with matched comparison group	12	50.0
Quasi-experiment with nonequivalent comparison group	9	37.5
Quasi-experiment with no comparison group (ITS)	3	12.5
Intervention Type		
Gang / group violence	12	50.0
Individual offender	3	12.5
Drug market	9	37.5
Displacement and Diffusion		
Measured displacement / diffusion	5	20.8
Did not measure displacement / diffusion	19	79.2
Publication Type		
Peer-reviewed journal	15	62.5
Grey literature	9	37.5
Published report	2	8.3
Unpublished report	7	29.2
Completion Year		
2001–2004	2	8.3
2005–2008	5	20.8
2009–2012	5	20.8
2013–2015	12	50.0

Note: ITS = Interrupted Time Series
Source: Braga, Weisburd, & Turchan (2018: 218).

studies were conducted in the United States. The evaluation evidence on the
effects of focused deterrence on crime is relatively new with all twenty-four
evaluations completed after 2000 and half released after 2013. Twelve evaluations tested the violence prevention impacts of GVI programs, nine evaluations
considered the effects of DMI programs on crime problems connected to street-

level drug markets, and three evaluations appraised crime reductions generated by focused deterrence programs targeting individual repeat offenders. The twenty-four studies included in the systematic review were:

1. Operation Ceasefire in Boston, Massachusetts (Braga et al., 2001)
2. Indianapolis Violence Reduction Partnership in Indianapolis, Indiana (McGarrell et al., 2006)
3. Operation Peacekeeper in Stockton, California (Braga, 2008b)
4. Project Safe Neighborhoods in Lowell, Massachusetts (Braga, Pierce, et al., 2008)
5. Cincinnati Initiative to Reduce Violence in Cincinnati, Ohio (Engel et al., 2010)
6. Operation Ceasefire in Newark, New Jersey (Boyle et al., 2010)
7. Operation Ceasefire in Los Angeles, California (Tita et al., 2004)
8. Operation Ceasefire in Rochester, New York (Delaney, 2006)
9. Project Safe Neighborhoods in Chicago, Illinois (Papachristos, Meares, & Fagan, 2007)
10. Drug Market Intervention in Rockford, Illinois (Corsaro, Brunson, & McGarrell, 2009)
11. Drug Market Intervention in Nashville, Tennessee (Corsaro, Brunson, & McGarrell, 2010)
12. Drug Market Intervention in High Point, North Carolina (Corsaro et al., 2012)
13. Drug Market Intervention in Peoria, Illinois (Corsaro & Brunson, 2013)
14. Operation Ceasefire II in Boston, Massachusetts (Braga, Hureau, & Papachristos, 2014)
15. Community Initiative to Reduce Violence in Glasgow, Scotland (Williams et al., 2014)
16. Group Violence Reduction Strategy in Chicago, Illinois (Papachristos & Kirk, 2015)
17. Group Violence Reduction Strategy in New Orleans, Louisiana (Corsaro & Engel, 2015)
18. No Violence Alliance in Kansas City, Missouri (Fox, Novak, & Yaghoub, 2015)
19. Project Longevity in New Haven, Connecticut (Sierra-Arevalo et al., 2015)
20. Drug Market Intervention in Roanoke, Virginia (Saunders, Kilmer, & Ober, 2015)
21. Drug Market Intervention in Montgomery County, Maryland (Saunders et al., 2015)
22. Drug Market Intervention in Guntersville, Alabama (Saunders et al., 2015)
23. Drug Market Intervention in Seattle, Washington (Saunders et al., 2015)

24. Drug Market Intervention in Ocala, Florida (Saunders et al., 2015)

All twenty-four studies used varying kinds of quasi-experimental designs to analyze the impact of focused deterrence strategies on crime (Braga, Weisburd, & Turchan, 2018). Rigorous quasi-experimental designs with near-equivalent comparison groups created through matching techniques were used in twelve evaluations (50 percent). Quasi-experimental designs with nonequivalent comparison groups based on naturally occurring conditions, such as other cities or within-city areas that did not receive treatment, were used in nine studies (37.5 percent). One-group-only interrupted time-series designs that used statistical controls to account for trends and seasonal variations were used in three evaluations (12.5 percent). The impacts of crime prevention programs can be limited if the implemented intervention results in crime displacement associated with the movement of criminal offenders to commit crime in other unprotected areas or at unprotected times, the commission of crime in new ways, or some other variation (see, e.g., Reppetto, 1976). Other scholars have observed that crime prevention programs can generate the opposite of displacement – a diffusion of crime control benefits to unprotected areas or targets – as potential criminals overestimate the reach of implemented programs (Clarke & Weisburd, 1994). Five focused deterrence studies included in the systematic review considered whether the evaluated program resulted in crime displacement or diffusion of crime control benefits.

Nineteen of the twenty-four focused deterrence evaluations (79.2 percent) included in the review reported at least one noteworthy crime control impact (Braga, Weisburd, & Turchan, 2018). Statistically significant crime reduction effects were found in all twelve evaluations of GVI programs, five of nine DMI programs, and two of three focused deterrence programs addressing violent behavior by individuals. No discernible crime reduction impacts were reported in four evaluations of DMI programs launched in Guntersville (AL), Montgomery County (MD), Ocala (FL), and Peoria (IL) (Saunders et al., 2015). The evaluation of the Newark (NJ) Operation Ceasefire focused deterrence strategy, which was applied to prevent gun violence by individual gang members in a targeted area, reported a non-statistically significant reduction in gunshot wounds in the target zone relative to a matched untreated area (Boyle et al., 2010).

None of the five studies that examined possible crime displacement effects noted significant movement of offending from targeted areas into surrounding areas or increased violence by untreated gangs socially connected to targeted gangs (Braga, Weisburd, & Turchan, 2018). Rather, three studies reported noteworthy diffusion of crime control benefits associated with the implementation of the focused deterrence strategies in targeted areas. The Nashville DMI study found that the intervention reduced drug crimes by 56 percent in the targeted McFerrin Park area and by 38 percent in an adjoining area (Corsaro, Brunson, & McGarrell, 2010). The Los Angeles Ceasefire GVI evaluation reported that violent crime had decreased by 34 percent, gang crime decreased by 28 percent, and gun crime decreased by 26 percent in targeted areas following the start of the intervention (Tita et al., 2004). In immediately proximate areas, violent crime had also decreased by 33 percent, gang crime decreased by 44 percent, and gun crime decreased by 28 percent after the Ceasefire program commenced in the targeted areas.

3.1.1 Meta-analysis of Crime Reduction Effects

The systematic review used meta-analysis to synthesize the crime reduction impacts across the twenty-four focused deterrence evaluations (Braga, Weisburd, & Turchan, 2018). The "effect size" statistic was used to represent the strength and direction (positive or negative) of each included study in the overall meta-analysis of included program evaluations, and the "mean effect size" represented the average effect of focused deterrence on reported crime outcomes across all included evaluations (Lipsey & Wilson, 2001). Effect sizes of .20 suggest small program impacts on outcomes, .50 suggest medium program impacts, and .80 suggest large program impacts (Cohen, 1988). Figure 4 presents the effect sizes and 95 percent confidence intervals for all included focused deterrence evaluations. The meta-analysis suggests that focused deterrence programs have an overall statistically significant moderate effect on crime (mean effect size = .383, $p < .05$).

The meta-analysis also considered whether differing types of focused deterrence programs generated similar effects on targeted crime problems (Braga, Weisburd, & Turchan, 2018). GVI focused deterrence programs were associated with the largest crime reduction impacts (.657, $p < .05$), while individual offender and DMI focused deterrence programs were associated with smaller impacts (.204 and .091, respectively; both $p < .05$). The review found that the smaller DMI effect sizes were influenced by program implementation fidelity issues. The four DMI program evaluations that reported implementation difficulties primarily stemming from a lack of community involvement in targeted drug market areas were associated with a very small mean effect size (.053, not statistically significant). In comparison, DMI programs that did not experience noteworthy implementation problems generated a more modest impact on crime in targeted areas (.184, $p < .05$).

An emerging policy consensus on the crime control value of these strategies has also been shaped by other systematic assessments of the growing body of evaluation evidence on the crime reduction impacts of focused deterrence programs. For instance, Abt and Winship (2016: 13) conducted a meta-

Mean Effect Sizes for Study Outcomes

Study name	Outcome	Std diff in means	Standard error	Std diff in means and 95% CI
Lowell PSN	Gun assaults	1.186	0.207	
Indianapolis VRS	Total homicides	1.039	0.283	
NH Longevity	Combined	0.936	0.324	
Nashville DMI	Combined	0.838	0.320	
Stockton, CA	Gun homicides	0.763	0.157	
Rochester Ceasefire	Combined	0.675	0.298	
NOLA GVRS	Combined	0.656	0.283	
Boston Ceasefire I	Combined	0.645	0.241	
KC NoVA	Combined	0.607	0.322	
LA Ceasefire	Combined	0.565	0.351	
Rockford DMI	Combined	0.521	0.285	
Boston Ceasefire II	Combined	0.503	0.068	
Chicago GVRS	Total gang shootings	0.414	0.157	
Cincinnati IRV	GMI homicides	0.352	0.224	
Glasgow CIRV	Combined	0.298	0.133	
Guntersville DMI	Combined	0.248	0.225	
High Point DMI	Combined	0.243	0.126	
Newark Ceasefire	Gun shot wounds	0.225	0.160	
Chicago PSN	Combined	0.181	0.061	
Roanoke DMI	Combined	0.079	0.082	
Seattle DMI	All crime	0.074	0.035	
Peoria DMI	Combined	0.037	0.300	
Ocala DMI	All crime	-0.001	0.055	
Montgomery DMI	All crime	-0.051	0.116	
		0.383	0.061	

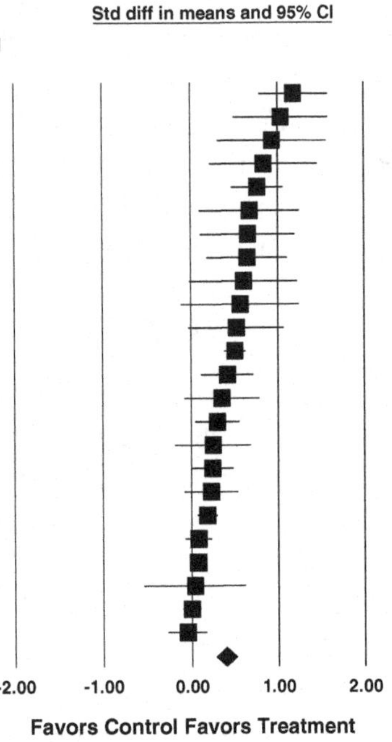

-2.00   -1.00   0.00   1.00   2.00

Favors Control Favors Treatment

Figure 4. Campbell Review Meta-analysis of Included Focused Deterrence Studies

Source: Braga, Weisburd, & Turchan (2018: 232).

analysis of 43 reviews including over 1,400 studies of community violence prevention programs and concluded that "Focused deterrence ... has the largest direct impact on crime and violence, of any intervention in this report." Likewise, Wong et al. (2012: 29) conducted a systematic review of strategies to control street gangs and reported that "'Pulling-levers' strategies ... are the most consistently effective solution to gang-related delinquency."

3.1.2 Increasingly Rigorous Program Evaluation Evidence

The general consensus that focused deterrence strategies generate notable crime prevention gains has been driven by increasingly rigorous evaluation methodologies being applied in program assessments. The first iteration of the review found that only 30 percent (3 of 10) of eligible studies used quasi-experimental designs with matched comparison groups (Braga & Weisburd, 2012). In contrast, 64.3 percent (9 of 14) of the newly identified studies in the most recent version of the review used these more rigorous controlled designs (Braga,

Weisburd, & Turchan, 2018). The trend toward quasi-experimental designs with higher levels of internal validity has influenced the confidence of outside reviewers of the evaluation evidence that focused deterrence programs do indeed reduce crime. For instance, the U.S. National Academies Committee to Review Research on Police Policy and Practices (Skogan & Frydl, 2004: 241) characterized the scientific evidence on focused deterrence programs as "descriptive rather than evaluative." Fourteen years later, as mentioned, the National Academies Committee on Proactive Policing (Weisburd & Majmundar, 2018: 7) stated that "focused deterrence programs generate statistically significant short- and long-term areawide crime reduction impacts."

Evaluations of the separate implementations of Operation Ceasefire in Boston during the 1990s and again in the mid-2000s provide examples of how the rigor of quasi-experimental evaluations has evolved over the last twenty years. The 1990s Ceasefire implementation was evaluated using a nonrandomized quasi-experiment that compared Boston youth homicide trends to youth homicide trends within other major U.S. cities (Braga et al., 2001). The cross-city comparison was supported by within-city time series analyses that compared pre- versus post-implementation trends in multiple serious violence outcomes including citywide youth homicides, citywide shots fired calls for service, citywide gun assaults, and youth gun assaults in one high-risk policing district. The within-city time series controlled for rival causal factors such as trends, seasonal variations, employment trends, youth population trends, and broader changes in violence over time. As described earlier, the evaluation estimated a 63 percent reduction in monthly counts of Boston youth homicides that was distinct from youth homicide trends in other U.S. cities and also reported significant reductions in the other within-city gun violence outcomes (Braga et al., 2001).

The 1990s Boston Ceasefire evaluation was a less rigorous quasi-experimental design. The U.S. National Academies Committee to Improve Research Information and Data on Firearms reviewed the 1990s Ceasefire evaluation and noted these methodological shortcomings. While the committee (Wellford, Pepper, & Petrie, 2005: 238) suggested that the evaluation was "compelling" in associating the youth homicide decline with the Ceasefire implementation, they observed that certain internal validity threats could not be ruled out such as complex interaction effects among the rival causal factors included in the analysis. More directly, the committee commented that the evaluation did not make direct links between key components of the focused deterrence program and subsequent changes in the violent behaviors of individuals subjected to the intervention (Wellford, Pepper, & Petrie, 2005).

The evaluation of the reconstituted Boston Ceasefire program implemented during the mid-2000s used a much stronger quasi-experimental evaluation design (Braga, Hureau, & Papachristos, 2014). In particular, the Ceasefire evaluation was explicitly designed to determine whether gangs exposed to the focused deterrence intervention subsequently changed their shooting behaviors. Boston gangs targeted by the Ceasefire treatment were statistically matched to untreated Boston gangs that were not connected to the Ceasefire gangs through rivalries or alliances. The Ceasefire impact was assessed via differences-in-differences estimators that compared gun violence trends for matched treatment gangs relative to gun violence trends for matched comparison gangs. The analysis suggested that total shootings involving directly treated gangs were reduced by 31 percent relative to total shootings involving comparison gangs over the course of the 2006 through 2010 study period (Figure 5).

A companion analysis used the same rigorous quasi-experimental design to determine whether the Ceasefire focused deterrence violence reduction impacts spilled over to untreated gangs that were socially connected to treated gangs through rivalries and alliances (Braga, Apel, & Welsh, 2013). Figure 6 illustrates the social connections among directly treated and "vicariously treated" gangs in a first-order social network clique centered on the treated Heath Street gang. The Academy Homes, Annunciation Road, Egleston Square, H-Block, and Walnut Park gangs had active rivalries with the Heath Street gang. The Bragdon Street and Lenox Street gangs had alliances with Heath Street. The

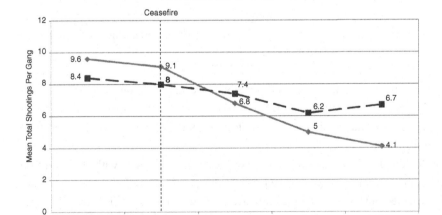

Figure 5. Main Effects of Mid-2000s Implementation of Boston Ceasefire.
Source: Braga, Hureau, & Papachristos (2014: 128).

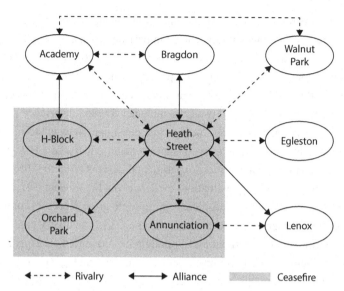

Figure 6. Heath Street Gang First-Order Clique of Rivals and Allies.
Source: Braga, Apel, & Welsh (2013: 325).

H-Block, Orchard Park, Annunciation Road, and Heath Street gangs were targeted by the Ceasefire program during the 2006–10 evaluation period. Although these gangs did not directly experience the Ceasefire program, the Academy Homes, Bragdon Street, Egleston Square, Lenox Street, and Walnut Park gangs may have altered their violent behaviors based on knowledge of what happened to their rivals and allies. The main effects evaluation excluded these untreated groups from the analysis because of treatment contamination concerns. However, the companion analysis focused on the shooting behaviors of these gangs to determine whether Ceasefire generated any spillover deterrent effects among these vicariously treated groups relative to comparison gangs that did not receive direct treatment and were not socially connected to targeted gangs. This study found that total shootings involving these vicariously treated gangs were reduced by 24 percent relative to total shooting involving matched comparison gangs.

A much more conservative violence reduction impact was estimated by the more rigorous quasi-experimental evaluation of the mid-2000s Boston Ceasefire implementation (31 percent) when compared to the less rigorous quasi-experimental evaluation of the 1990s Boston Ceasefire implementation (63 percent). Similarly, the meta-analysis in the first iteration of the systematic review estimated a larger overall mean effect size (.604; Braga & Weisburd, 2012) relative to the most-recent version of the meta-analysis (.383; Braga, Weisburd, & Turchan, 2018). This difference in the overall mean effect size across the two reviews is due to the increased prevalence of stronger quasi-experimental evaluations with matched comparison groups. Studies with more rigorous evaluation designs tend to report null effects (Rossi, 1987) and often yield more conservative estimates of program impacts (Weisburd, Lum, & Petrosino, 2001). As suggested by the most recent review, this was certainly the case with the varying quality of the included focused deterrence program evaluations. As Figure 7 reveals, the matched quasi-experimental designs were associated with a much smaller within-group mean effect size (.194, p <.05) relative to the nonequivalent quasi-experimental designs (.703, p <.05).

The rigorous program evaluation evidence on the impacts of focused deterrence on targeted crime problems continues to grow. Recently completed rigorous quasi-experimental evaluations of the GVI in two very challenging urban environments – Oakland and Philadelphia – reported statistically significant reductions in shootings in areas with targeted gangs relative to matched comparison areas with untreated gangs (Braga et al., 2019; Roman, Link, et al., 2019). The Oakland quasi-experiment also examined the main and spillover focused deterrence impacts on total shootings involving treated gangs and vicariously treated gangs connected to targeted gangs through rivalries and alliances relative to total shootings by matched comparison gangs. The Oakland study reported the GVI reduced total shootings by more than 25 percent for both directly treated and vicariously treated gangs relative to matched comparison gangs (Braga et al., 2019). The Philadelphia quasi-experiment reported mixed findings at the gang level (Roman, Link, et al., 2019). Significant reductions in shootings were observed in turf areas surrounding treated gangs relative to turf areas of matched gangs; however, simple pre-post comparisons of gang-involved shootings by treated gangs did not show evidence of GVI impact. Roman, Link, et al. (2019) speculated that the divergent findings might be due to a less intensive GVI implementation, not measuring possible spillover effects to comparison gangs, and other factors.

Additional rigorous evaluations show impact from focused deterrence. Wood and Papachristos (2019) used social network analysis and quasi-experimental techniques to evaluate the direct and spillover effects of the Chicago PSN intervention on gunshot victimization of program participants and their untreated socially connected peers; they found that participation in the program reduced gunshot victimization for both groups over a two year post-treatment period. A quasi-experimental evaluation of Chicago PSN-style call-ins in another city, using a synthetic control design, found substantial crime reductions, including statistically significant reductions of 21 percent in gun robberies, 16 percent reduction in gun assaults, and 29 percent reduction in nongun

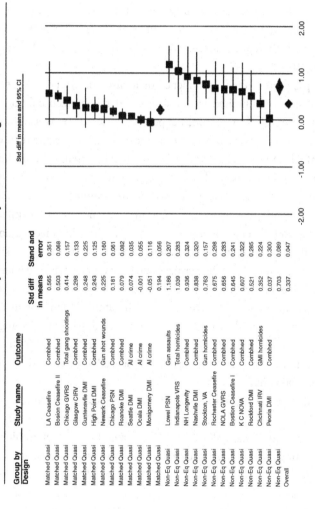

Mean Effect Sizes for Study Outcomes by Research Design

Figure 7. Campbell Review Meta-analysis of Included Focused Deterrence Studies by Rigor of Evaluation Design

Source: Braga, Weisburd, & Turchan (2018: 235).

robberies (Clark-Moorman, Rydberg, & McGarrell, 2019). And while the GVI call-ins are primarily designed to influence group activity and not primarily the behavior of the individual group members called in, research has in fact found substantial reductions in recidivism amongst call-in participants, particularly – as intended – for serious violent crime (Circo et al., 2019). Evaluations are also beginning the important work of unpacking the "black box" of the interventions. A study of GVI enforcement activities found that violence reductions were not associated with enhanced use of criminal justice sanctions, adding to earlier findings that the approach is not dependent on enhanced enforcement and can in fact lead to greatly reduced arrests (Roman, Forney, et al., 2019; Engel, Corsaro, & Ozer, 2017).

The available program evaluation evidence of focused deterrence has been previously characterized as limited by an absence of randomized controlled trials (Skogan & Frydl, 2004; Wellford, Pepper, & Petrie, 2005; Weisburd & Majmundar, 2018). After the completion of the most recent systematic review, Hamilton, Rosenfeld, and Levin (2018) finished the first randomized controlled trial of an individual offender focused deterrence program centered on reducing subsequent recidivism by high-risk probationers and parolees in St. Louis (MO). Probationers and parolees were randomly assigned to a treatment group that was invited to attend a focused deterrence notification meeting and a control group that was not invited to attend a notification meeting. The randomized experiment found that the parolees and probationers who did attend the focused deterrence notification meeting were less likely to be arrested over the following seventeen months relative to those who did not attend the meeting. Hamilton, Rosenfeld and Levin (2018: 14) concluded, "The results align with those of prior evaluations of individual-level focused deterrence initiatives indicating that the notification meeting, the crux of focused deterrence, serves to reduce future criminal behavior."

Nevertheless, there remains a clear need for more randomized experimental evaluations of focused deterrence programs. Future evaluations of focused deterrence programs addressing individual offender and drug market problems could draw on existing randomized experimental designs such as those used in the Hawaii Opportunity with Probation Enforcement (HOPE) evaluation (Hawken & Kleiman, 2009), Jersey City Drug Market Analysis Program evaluation (Weisburd & Green, 1995), and other randomized controlled trials. Randomized evaluations of GVI programs, however, are complicated by the use of interventions designed to generate spillover effects that could, in turn, contaminate control gangs, groups, and areas. Braga and Weisburd (2014) suggest that multisite cluster randomized trial designs could be used to conduct more rigorous evaluations of GVI programs. The random allocation of clusters of gangs connected by rivalries and alliances to treatment and control conditions could limit treatment contamination problems and facilitate a much-needed randomized controlled trial of the GVI.

4 Theoretical Perspectives Supporting Focused Deterrence

Theoretical perspectives on effective crime prevention principles in focused deterrence strategies offer further support to the existing evaluation evidence on the crime reduction benefits of focused deterrence strategies. In this section, we show that focused deterrence is bolstered by a strong logic model that adds considerable weight to the findings of existing program evaluations. While the existing empirical evidence doesn't directly evaluate these theoretical mechanisms, focused deterrence evaluations do provide insight into the impacts of these preventive actions that generate knowledge that aids the design of effective programs (see, e.g., Ludwig, Kling, & Mullainathan, 2011).

4.1 Getting Deterrence Right

Deterrence is based on a very simple and familiar framework: like other people, offenders and potential offenders pursue rewards and seek to avoid losses (Kennedy, 2008). Acts that carry penalties are less attractive than those that do not. When penalties are applied more reliably, more quickly, and with greater severity, specific acts become even less attractive. Deterrence theory suggests that, when offenders consider the costs of criminal acts to be greater than the benefits of those acts, crimes can be prevented (Zimring & Hawkins, 1973). Two distinct types of deterrence mechanisms are generally recognized in the existing literature: general deterrence and specific deterrence (Cook, 1980). General deterrence suggests that the broader population is discouraged from committing crimes when people see that sanctions follow criminal acts. Specific deterrence suggests that offenders are dissuaded from committing future crimes after sanctions follow their current offense. Punishments that are excessive, poorly motivated, and not well aligned with individual and community norms can be viewed as illegitimate (Kennedy, Kleiman, & Braga, 2017). The application of sanctions should be viewed as consistent with community and individual norms rather than threats wielded by external and possibly hostile authorities. Research on deterrence mechanisms has generally considered whether changing the severity, swiftness, and certainty of punishment for specific crimes influences the occurrence of those crimes (Nagin, 2013). Focused deterrence theory has added to this, in particular, considerations of the application of deterrence to groups and networks in addition to individuals; the role of communication; the role of nonlegal sanctions; the role of informal social control; and the role of communication.

Focused deterrence strategies represent a new approach to generating deterrent impacts as it attempts to make the prospect of sanctions more legitimate by bringing in individual norms, values, and informal social control (Kennedy 1997, 2009; Kleiman, 2009). Consistent with the views of many deterrence scholars (e.g., Zimring & Hawkins, 1973; Wilson, 1975; Cook, 1980; Nagin, 2013), a central component of the approach involves a shift away from severity and toward the swiftness and certainty of punishments. Clumsy, unfocused, and excessive punishment risks offender and community resistance and, as a purely practical matter, it is impossible to deliver more sanctions in an environment where overly harsh sanctions are routinely handed out in a nonstrategic manner. This results in both high violations rates and large volume of punishment – a result that is both toxic and routine in many high-crime urban neighborhoods (Kleiman, 2009).

The salience of prompt punishment was first recognized by Caesare Beccaria (1764/1872), who is generally recognized as the father of deterrence theory, centuries ago. He further recognized that offenders were not perfectly rational actors in the economic sense and were generally poor calculators of sanction risks. Offenders tend both to overvalue available and immediate rewards and discount distal and uncertain punishments. As such, increasing the severity of punishment is not a good substitute for swiftness and certainty in deterrence-based crime prevention strategies. In fact, increasing punishment severity can be counterproductive. James Q. Wilson (1975) observed that severity makes swiftness and certainty not feasible as harsh sanctions (such as long prison sentences) are expensive and difficult to impose consistently. Harsh punishments are not swift and certain as these sanctions are taken more seriously by authorities, communities, and offenders; have layers of procedural protections to avoid miscarriages of justice; and are opposed by the accused through a vigorous defense. Excessive punishments, in practice, work counter to effective deterrence principles.

Focused deterrence strategies economize on the severity of sanctions by imposing sanctions that are only as effective as needed to change very specific individual behaviors (Kennedy, 2008). Focused deterrence strategies place a premium on achieving fair, swift, and certain sanctions to generate crime control impacts. In particular, the approach attempts to generate swifter and more certain sanctions by focusing on a subset of offenses and offenders. By doing so, authorities have sufficient capacity to deliver an immediate law enforcement response to violations of set rules (e.g., don't shoot rival gang members) even in environments with high offending rates (Kennedy, Kleiman, & Braga, 2017). A valuable positive feedback loop can then be created as reduced rule violations result in diminished applications of law enforcement. This allows authorities to expand their focus to other offenders or offense types while maintaining their capacity to deliver a credible deterrence message to offenders.

A key element of focused deterrence strategies involves the delivery of a direct and explicit "retail deterrence" message to a relatively small target audience regarding what kind of behavior would provoke a special response and what that response would be (Kennedy, 2008). For instance, beyond the particular groups subjected to gang violence reduction sanctions the deterrence message was applied to a relatively small audience (e.g., all gang-involved youth in a particular city) rather than a general audience, and operated by making explicit cause-and-effect connections between the behavior of the target population and the behavior of the authorities. Knowledge of what happened to others in the target population was intended to prevent further acts of violence by gangs in the jurisdiction. The available research suggests that deterrent effects are ultimately determined by offender perceptions of sanction risk and certainty (Nagin, 2013). Durlauf and Nagin (2011: 40) observe, "strategies that result in large and visible shifts in apprehension risk are most likely to have deterrent effects that are large enough not only to reduce crime but also apprehensions" and identified focused deterrence strategies as having these characteristics.

Bentham's (1789/1988) sanction typology suggests there are five sources of "pain" that influence offenders' decisions to commit crimes: the physical sanction, the political sanction, the moral sanction, the religious sanction, and the sympathetic sanction. Although these kinds of sanctions are separate, their effects are intrinsically connected. Applying Bentham's typology to focused deterrence rests on the notion that his sanction types are compatible and work together to create the desired deterrent effect. With the obvious exclusion of applying physical sanctions (which involve torture), focused deterrence strategies can be viewed as an exercise in optimizing the possible impacts of these varied kinds of sanctions levied toward changing offender perceptions of continuing their criminal behavior. This is most directly the case with the strategic application of political sanctions, or the punishment of individuals by government officials. However, the inclusion of the other three sanction types in the strategy may also serve to enhance crime prevention efficacy of focused deterrence.

Focused deterrence strategies attempt to deter offenders from continuing to commit very specific types of criminal behaviors (e.g., gang-involved gun violence, disorderly street-level drug sales) by increasing the certainty and swiftness in the application of political sanctions. However, focused deterrence strategies are explicitly designed to prevent crime through the advertising of sanctions, and the personalized application of deterrence messages through direct meetings with identified individuals. The effective communication of sanctions to relevant audiences is an important step in generating deterrent impacts. As Zimring and Hawkins (1973: 142) observe, "the deterrence threat may best be viewed as a form of advertising." The approach directly engages offenders via group notification meetings (i.e., call-ins, forums) and customized individual notifications where criminal justice officials inform them that continued offending will not be tolerated and how the system will respond to violations of these new behavior standards. Direct communications, coupled with swift and certain sanctions for violating established behavioral norms, influence offender perceptions of apprehension risk. Face-to-face meetings with offenders are an important first step in altering their perceptions about sanction risk (Horney & Marshall, 1992; Nagin, 2013). As McGarrell et al. (2006) suggest, direct communications and affirmative follow-up responses are the types of new information that may cause offenders to reassess the risks of continuing their criminal behavior.

The delivery of direct and specific information about sanction risks, rather than inferences about actual official actions based on personal or vicarious experiences, can further reduce the need for actual punishment (Kennedy, Kleiman, & Braga, 2017). Inferences can overestimate and underestimate actual sanction risks. Even in relatively stable sanction environments, it may be too late for offenders to adapt their behaviors given that law enforcement agencies constantly change their priorities as new crime problems emerge, known offenders commit new crimes, and particular neighborhoods experience elevated victimization. Offender perceptions of sanction risks and certainty can be brought in line with law enforcement reality through direct communications. In turn, the effective delivery of the deterrence message can, theoretically and practically, substitute for on-the-ground enforcement and reduce the amount of actual sanction needed to address a recurring crime problem.

Direct communications with offenders also facilitate the elevation of moral norms by community members, religious norms by clergy members representing community interests, and sympathetic norms tied to the pain inflicted on others. During offender notification meetings, community members convey the harms to neighborhoods and residents generated by continued violent behavior, clergy describe the intense regret and long-lasting personal anguish they will experience for violating religious commandments against harming others, and mothers of victims communicate the intense loss they feel over losing their children to seemingly senseless violence (Kennedy, Kleiman, & Braga, 2017). The explicit inclusion of these other sources of "pain" complement the imposition of political sanctions to influence offender decisions to commit crimes. In fact, these norm-elevating conversations may be equally, if not more, powerful than the prospects of facing formal sanctions (Kennedy, 2008).

Criminologists have previously recognized the role that moral beliefs play in the deterrent effects of informal sanctions on criminal behavior. Grasmick and Bursik (1990) examined the impact of significant others and conscience on petty offending, and characterized costs as embarrassment and shame, respectively. They found shame to be a meaningful deterrent to tax offending, drunk driving, and minor theft; surprisingly, shame was a more powerful deterrent than formal sanctions for tax offending and drunk driving. In their examination of a range of minor offenses committed by high school and college students, Paternoster et al. (1983) found deterrent effects for "moral commitment" and "social disapproval." In a scenario study of sexual offending, Bachman, Paternoster, and Ward (1992) reported an impact from the risk of formal sanctions only when respondents did not find the described assault as innately morally reprehensible. In all other scenarios, moral inhibitions toward sexual assault were a much more powerful deterrent than formal sanctions or the disapproval of others. Moral repugnance for *mala in se* crimes (reprehensible crimes such as murder and rape) may make formal sanctions not necessary to influence the behavior of most people (Williams & Hawkins, 1986).

Partnering criminal justice agencies frame deterrent messages to address the group or other collective context from which many crime problems emerge. Indeed, gang activity involves not only relationships within groups but relationships among networks of groups (see, e.g., Papachristos, Hureau, & Braga, 2013), as does, in a different sense, drug market activity and many other important crime problems. While this is a common notion in other settings – deterrence in international relations is conceived of as between, for example, opposing nations or militaries, not individual politicians or soldiers – the habit of mind in criminology and crime prevention has overwhelmingly been about individuals. There is no good theoretical or practical reason for this. Group behavior is not reducible to the aggregation of individual dispositions and decisions. In focused deterrence, the groups themselves can also act as another internal communication vehicle for transmitting the actual sanction risk to other offenders (Kennedy, 2008). Sanctions for particular acts are applied to groups; all communications to offenders focus on this group concept, with the thought that peer pressure will change individual and group behavior. As Braga and Kennedy (2012) describe, meaningful enforcement actions and scrutiny by law enforcement agencies can leverage the rationality of group members to no longer encourage norms that provoke the outbreaks of violence.

The citywide communication of the anti-violence message, coupled with meaningful examples of the consequences that will be brought to bear on groups that break the rules, can weaken or eliminate the "kill or be killed" norm as individuals recognize that their enemies will be operating under the new rules as well. Changes in group norms and in objective risks associated with particular forms of misbehavior may, for example, make it more difficult to recruit peers for particular instances of co-offending. Ethnographic research on illicit gun markets in Chicago has shown that gangs' assessment of the law enforcement responses to gun violence leads them to withhold access to firearms for younger and more impulsive members (Cook et al., 2007). DMI's goal of fundamentally disrupting overt drug markets can greatly enhance the difficulty of drug dealing: when buyers no longer routinely "cruise" once-active markets, even a motivated street dealer may find it impossible to do business, and the authorities' openly declared focus on the geographic market can be enough to keep dealers and buyers away (Kennedy & Wong, 2009; Kennedy, 1990). Persistent enforcement directed at geographically defined illicit drug markets may have no impact on the underlying problem – dealers are readily replaced even as new users present themselves – while disruption of the connection between dealers and buyers may lead to the collapse of the market (Kleiman, 2009; Kennedy, 2009a). A focused deterrence approach to intimate partner violence predicated on communicating and ensuring "pulling levers" attention to the most dangerous offenders, while communicating that focus and intent to less dangerous offenders, appears to have curbed both the most dangerous abuse and overall intimate partner recidivism (Sechrist & Weil, 2018).

As described earlier, the offender notification sessions in the Chicago PSN strategy were associated with the largest violence reduction impacts of the varied components of that focused deterrence intervention (Papachristos, Meares, & Fagan, 2007). A recently completed randomized experiment tested three crime prevention mechanisms involved in the Chicago PSN offender notification meetings – perceptions of risks associated with future offending, perceptions of police legitimacy, and adherence to community norms (Trinkner, 2019). Over the course of a one-year period, parolees participating in the PSN program were randomly assigned to complete surveys on these mechanisms either before the offender notification meeting (control group) or immediately after the meeting (treatment group). The randomized experiment revealed that treatment parolees reported significantly increased perceptions of apprehension risks following the offender notification meetings (Trinkner, 2019). This suggests that focused deterrence communication strategies do indeed influence targeted offenders regarding the law enforcement risks associated with continuing their criminal behavior. The study did not find any differences in parolee perceptions of adherence to community norms when the treatment and control groups were compared. However, relative to the perceptions of control parolees, treatment parolees perceived the police to be more legitimate authorities and were more likely to judge the police as procedurally fair (Trinkner, 2019). The implications of these findings are considered in the next section.

The condition of chronicity and wide-ranging offending is not essential to either deterrence in general or focused deterrence in particular; both could still operate if, for example, group members and the most serious domestic violence offenders were not frequently also chronic offenders both within and across offense categories. But since that is in fact the case, it is also the case that such high-risk groups and individuals are singularly susceptible to "pulling levers" interventions – they can in fact be sanctioned for particular offenses through strategic attention to their other offending behavior. That fact, properly mobilized, means that such particularly serious groups and individuals can be met with greatly enhanced certainty and swiftness, and that that can be communicated to them ahead of time in ways designed to mobilize both their and their wider community's norms. The most serious and chronic offenders can thus be seen to be distinctively open to deterrence, rather than – as is usually the case – distinctively impervious or resistant.

4.2 Promoting Legitimacy and Procedural Justice

Focused deterrence builds upon concepts of police legitimacy and procedural justice. More than just public support, legitimacy represents the willingness of the public to recognize and voluntarily defer to official authority (Beetham, 1991). As with the working of informal social control, legitimacy produces public safety and reduces crime without the actual exercise of state power. Beyond that, police work is much easier when citizens voluntarily support the police by sharing information on crimes, cooperating with crime prevention initiatives, and complying with officer instructions (Meares & Kahan, 1998). A number of factors, such as crime control effectiveness, the equitable distribution of resources, and procedural fairness, have been found to be associated with citizen perceptions of police legitimacy (Bottoms & Tankebe, 2012; Jackson & Bradford, 2009; Reisig et al., 2007). Focused deterrence can improve citizen perceptions of the equitable distribution of police resources through its tight focus on high-rate offenders currently engaged in persistent crime problems and police crime control efficacy via its demonstrated crime reduction gains. However, the strategy's most powerful impacts on citizen perceptions of police legitimacy and procedural justice might be achieved through its direct communications with offenders. As described previously, high-risk offenders are warned of the enforcement consequences associated with continued violent behavior and are encouraged to take advantage of services and opportunities being offered to them. In the eyes of community members, there is an inherent fairness in offering identified offenders a choice and providing resources to support their transition away from violent behavior rather than simply arresting and prosecuting them.

Citizens view criminal justice institutions as legitimate when these organizations and their individual actors apply the laws and rules that govern public conduct in an appropriate manner (Sunshine & Tyler, 2003). Research suggests that public views of the police are strongly influenced by police behavior and citizens are responsive to the manner in which the police exercise their authority (Tyler, 2006). As such, the procedural justice of police actions in their encounters with citizens has been suggested to shape public perceptions of police legitimacy in powerful ways for both white and minority citizens (Tyler, 2006). Unfair policing practices, such as racially disparate and indiscriminate enforcement exercises, decrease citizen views of police legitimacy and undermine their ability to operate in affected communities (Fagan, 2002; Tyler & Wakslak, 2004). Comparative research in other countries report similar findings (e.g., Jonathan-Zamir & Weisburd, 2013; Tankebe, 2013). In essence, procedurally just encounters can enhance community member cooperation and compliance; in turn, this improves the efficacy of police work in communities.

The process-based model of police legitimacy suggests that citizens' assessments of the police are directly and measurably influenced by the way police treat citizens (Tyler, 2003). Police are viewed as legitimate authorities when citizens perceive that the police treat citizens with respect and make their decisions to use authority fairly. When this occurs, citizens are more likely to comply with the law and cooperate with police. As such, there are two associated elements used by citizens to determine procedural justice in police-citizen interactions: quality of decision making (e.g., officer decisions were based on objective indicators) and quality of treatment (e.g., citizens were treated with dignity and respect) (Tyler, 2003; Reisig et al., 2007). The key components of the process-based model of police legitimacy have been supported by a number of nonexperimental studies (see, e.g., Paternoster et al., 1997; Sunshine & Tyler, 2003; Tyler & Wakslak, 2004). Nagin and Telep (2017), however, suggest that the available empirical evidence is not strong enough to warrant causal inferences between procedural justice and citizen compliance with the law (see also Worden & McLean, 2017).

Offender notification meetings are administered according to the two key elements of the process-based model. First, establishing quality decision making, the identification of the group for the focused intervention is justified to the offenders in the room. It is important for the attending offenders to understand that they were selected for intervention because of their behavior (e.g., disorderly street-level drug sales that are harming the vitality of their community) rather than their status (e.g., street-level drug dealers who live in a disadvantaged neighbor-hood with very limited economic opportunities). Second, promoting quality of treatment, the partnership expresses concern for the well-being of the community and of the offenders themselves and offers offenders a clear choice in a respectful and business-like manner. This simple message is often framed as, "We'll help you if you let us, and we'll stop you if you make us." Law enforcement officials promote accountability by spelling out the group consequences for continued offending by its members while community members and service providers promise support and assistance.

Focused deterrence programs promote views of offenders as not inherently bad people even if some of them have committed heinous acts; as not driven by intrinsically poor character but by ongoing risk, fear, trauma, and confusion; as making unfortunate decisions that are motivated in part by incoherent official structures and actions rather than a desire for bad consequences; as often acting seemingly irrationally but still primarily rational; and as not monstrous but quite human (Kennedy, Kleiman, & Braga, 2017). By taking this view, focused deterrence emphasizes developing an understanding of who offenders are and why they behave in particular ways; treating them with respect; offering them protection and support; displaying empathy and compassion; assisting them to understand how and why sanctions are delivered and how to avoid being sanctioned; and, when sanctions are needed, representing the actions of law enforcement as based on objective reasons rather than personal in nature. Incorporating these conceptions into communications with offenders and com-munity residents alike positions participating criminal justice agencies as fair and trustworthy authorities.

Practical and theoretical work in procedural justice and legitimacy has significantly improved the setting, tone, and content of direct communication with offenders. This work has guided the selection of venues where communi-cations occur, emphasizing places considered locations of civic importance – such as community centers, churches, and black-history museums – instead of formal criminal justice settings such as courtrooms (Meares, 2009). Procedural justice and legitimacy concepts have influenced the staging of events in these places by using equitable in-the-round seating arrangements rather than more traditional, linear, dominant/subordinate seating provisions (Papachristos, Meares, & Fagan, 2007). These ideals have underscored the need for respectful communication, and driven sometimes stark changes in content: once unrelent-ingly uncompromising law enforcement officials expressing sympathy and understanding for offenders, emphasizing the desire to keep them safe and for their success, admitting and even apologizing for past attitudes and actions, and even addressing and condemning the role of law enforcement in racial oppression (Kennedy, 2009a; Mentel, 2012).

Illegitimate and ineffective criminal justice responses to offending can exacerbate crime problems in minority communities. Developing research on legal cynicism – a cultural orientation in which the agents of the law (police, prosecution, and corrections) are viewed as ineffective and illegitimate – suggests that people who hold these views feel freer to violate the law (Sampson & Bartusch, 1998; Kirk & Papachristos, 2011). This perspective has been expanded to a more serious diagnosis in disadvantaged neighborhoods suffering from serious crime problems: the legal estrangement of people of color. According to Bell (2017: 2054), legal estrangement is "a theory of detachment and eventual alienation from the law's enforcers, and it reflects the intuition among many people in poor communities of color that the law operates to exclude them from society." Minority citizens struggle with the consequences of balancing a strong need for effective crime prevention approaches while, at the same time, being uncertain whether the police are truly interested in controlling crime in their neighborhoods due to basic concerns about the problematic nature of many police-minority citizen encounters (e.g., see Bell, 2016, 2017; Brunson, 2007).

Law enforcement authorities in some focused deterrence strategies attempt to diminish legal cynicism and estrangement not only by demonstrating that they care about offenders, their families, and their communities but also by launching "police-community reconciliation" engagement. This work involves law enforcement directly acknowledging past and present harms, centering community experiences and narratives, and taking concrete steps to repair existing and prevent future harms (Kennedy and Ben-Menachem, 2019; Kennedy, 2009a; Mentel, 2012). In settings with a sharp divide between law enforcement agencies and minority communities, it may be a critical initial move toward building the trust and partnership needed to establish legitimacy and working relationships. Indeed, in High Point (NC), it was not possible to garner the community support needed to launch the DMI until these conversations were held (Kennedy, 2009a: 15, 17):

> Racial dynamics . . . created a brick wall that precludes meaningful conversations. The key to getting through that brick wall in High Point turned out to be telling the truth. You cannot get rid of history, but you can face facts, tell the truth, and find a way to move forward.
>
> We found that when we discussed race in the context of a core community issue – drug markets – we could make progress because everyone agreed on the basics.

There is very limited research evidence about the impact of procedural justice and legitimacy-building efforts within focused deterrence strategies. Offenders who participate in call-in sessions seem to notice the positive difference in messaging by law enforcement officials (Trinkner, 2019). And certain program implementers and evaluators also seemed convinced that the inclusion of these principles matters a great deal (Papachristos, Meares, & Fagan, 2007; Wallace et al., 2016). As described by Kennedy, Kleiman, and Braga (2017: 169), those involved in GVI interventions have felt a meaningful difference in practice when criminal justice authorities say, on the one hand, "I know who you are, I know what you're doing, and if you kill somebody I'll come at you with everything I've got," and those who say, on the other, "I care about you, I care about your families, I know what we've been doing has not been keeping you safe, and I will do everything in my power to keep you alive, unhurt, and out of jail." For most offenders from and residents of disadvantaged mostly minority neighborhoods, this is a very different message from law enforcement officials on how they intend to enhance public safety.

4.3 Mobilizing Informal Social Control

Social disorganization theory suggests that neighborhood crime variations within cities are influenced by community-level structural factors, such as relative deprivation, population turnover, and a lack of economic opportunity, and mediated by informal social controls representing the reactions of community members and groups that influence individual adherence to laws and prosocial norms (Shaw & McKay, 1942; Bursik & Grasmick, 1993). Conceptions of informal social control in neighborhoods have been further developed by the idea of collective efficacy, which is generally defined as "social cohesion among neighbors combined with their willingness to intervene on behalf of the common good" (Sampson, Raudenbush, & Earls, 1997: 918). Concentrated disadvantage in communities, which represents challenges such as elevated levels of unemployment, poverty, female-headed households, and individuals on public assistance, undermines the capacity of residents to develop collective efficacy. Neighborhoods characterized by high levels of violence are generally characterized by increased concentrated disadvantage and diminished collective efficacy (Sampson, Raudenbush, & Earls, 1997).

Informal social control – individual norms, conscience, and shame; the influence of one's own family, friends, and social network; and broad community norms and standards – is more powerful (because more legitimate, ubiquitous, and immediate) than formal social control as exercised by criminal justice authorities and institutions (Kennedy, Kleiman, & Braga, 2017,

Kennedy 2016). Social organization and the capacity of residents to exert informal social control over public places helps to prevent community violence (Bursik & Grasmick, 1993). Collective efficacy and collective civic action are promoted by the existence of community-based organizations comprising individuals who both come from outside and reside within particular communities (Sampson, 2012). The well-being of larger neighborhood areas is ensured by a range of organizations such as community newspapers, family planning clinics, alcohol/drug treatment centers, counseling or mentoring services (e.g., Big Brother), neighborhood watch, and other local agencies. An important element of fostering informal social controls involves increasing positive connections between youth and adults in the neighborhood. These improved connections can be fostered through programs that increase parent involvement in after-school and nighttime youth activities, adult-youth mentoring systems, and organized adult supervision of youth leisure-time activities (Sampson, 2012).

Community-based organizations and resident groups can be potent crime prevention partners for law enforcement agencies. Focused deterrence programs seek to stimulate informal social control crime prevention mechanisms to reduce both offending rates and punishment rates. These programs customarily include relevant community-based organizations in the larger crime reduction partnership to participate in operational decision making and deliver key intervention actions. For instance, in the Ceasefire GVI, Boston Ten Point Coalition activist black clergy helped police by mobilizing local communities to act against violence through peace walks and other public events, sharing information on the underlying nature of ongoing disputes between rival gangs with law enforcement agencies, communicating the anti-violence message during call-ins and throughout the city, and appealing to gang youth and their families to take advantage of services and opportunities rather than persisting in high-risk activities (Brunson et al., 2015).

Many of these measures may appear, at face value, to be fairly standard informal social control actions. However, one key theoretical and practical idea in focused deterrence is in direct opposition to mainstream ideas about "dangerous" individuals and communities. Rather than attempting to change presumed antisocial norms and values, focused deterrence recognizes the prevalence of powerful prosocial norms and seeks to elevate them (Kennedy, Kleiman, & Braga, 2017). Despite appearances and the views of outsiders, potential offenders' own norms and values may not be as deviant or oppositional as is usually supposed; their offending behavior may not in fact be in alignment with those norms and values; and their own thinking may be remarkably mainstream.

Pluralistic ignorance, as described earlier, readily allows for group members to believe that all members believe what none in fact believes, and to conform individual behavior to that faux norm (Matza, 1964). Individuals may act out of similarly mistaken notions of broader community norms, or adhere to real norms to which they do not personally subscribe; be pressured into action by both enemies and friends; be put in positions they do not like, for example feeling that they cannot ask authorities for help; or in various other ways end up acting in ways that do not reflect their own values and preferences. Research evidence supports this idea: even serious offenders frequently express such things as that killing is wrong, that they are doing what they are doing because their friends are making them, that they have to act violently because the police don't care and won't help, and the like. Research into attitudes of violent and gun offenders has found quite mainstream views about obeying the law combined with high levels of distrust for the police (Papachristos, Meares, & Fagan, 2012), while ethnographies of gang members frequently find them feeling more pressured and trapped than committed (Pitts, 2007).

This crime prevention orientation places a premium on identifying the community members whose roles and actions would be respected and attended to by the high-risk populations (Kennedy, Kleiman, & Braga, 2017). Every such population of potential offenders has such figures it respects, and it has proven possible in practice to find figures willing and even eager to play that role. When officials actually investigate the question "Who will the potential offenders listen to?" rather than assuming that they already know the answer, they often are surprised. The key figures will be different in different settings, but once the basic question is asked – Who will those whose behavior we're trying to change listen to? – it turns out to be answerable. In GVI, it has consistently been surviving mothers of murdered gang members; older and wiser "OGs," or "original gangsters," who've turned their lives around; and various community faith leaders and elders (Braga et al., 2019). Drug market interventions have engaged respected members of the community whose lives have been disrupted, property values damaged, children driven away, and the like. They even engage drug dealers' own family members, who both care about them and suffer when, for example, they are hurt or jailed; violence is directed at family members and homes; or dealers' illegal activity threatens parents' home ownership, tenant status, or jobs (Kennedy & Wong, 2009). In particular settings like the city of St. Paul, Minnesota's "*No Mas*" intervention with Latino gang members, the role was filled by officials of the Mexican government who articulated that gang offending would bring deeply unwanted immigration enforcement attention on the larger community, and community elders who articulated that gang members' obsession with an ersatz "respect" was in direct contradiction to a real respect the community had built up over generations (Densley & Squier Jones, 2016).

A particularly important role has been framed as that of the "influential": a person already in a given potential offender's social network whom they respect, who cares about them, and who can provide sustained positive influence (Kennedy & Wong, 2009). Such figures tend to be close family members but can include friends, romantic partners, faith leaders, coaches, and others. Workable ways of identifying influentials have been developed and include looking at formal criminal justice records – probation and parole reports, jail and prison visitation logs, jail and prison telephone logs – debriefing knowledgeable front-line criminal justice practitioners; and simply asking the potential offender in question. Involving influentials in engagements between potential offenders and the focused deterrence partnership has been an important part of many larger interventions.

"Outreach workers" or "streetworkers" have similarly frequently played an important role. Outreach workers are generally, though not always, former offenders who can build direct relationships with potential offender groups and individuals; dampen disputes; prevent retaliation; deflate the rumors and street dynamics that often drive violence; broker truces; ease access to social services; undercut and offer alternatives to the "street code" that drives crime and violence; and provide a safe and discreet way to carry messages to and from law enforcement. A long history of formal evaluation of "detached" outreach workers, operating in deliberate separation from and even opposition to law enforcement, shows the possibility of unintended criminogenic consequences (Klein, 2011). In the right roles and relationships, however, outreach workers have been important additions to community crime control capacity and important elements of successful focused deterrence interventions (Kennedy, 2009b).

There are other ways that focused deterrence programs attempt to mobilize informal social control mechanisms, such as by setting rules and engaging place managers, to deal with targeted crime problems. These approaches, however, are more consistent with crime opportunity theories, such as routine activity (Cohen & Felson, 1979) and rational choice (Cornish & Clarke, 1986), than social disorganization perspectives. Some scholars have suggested that social disorganization and routine activity theories are complementary and should be integrated (Miethe & Meier, 1994). For instance, the idea of increasing adult-youth connections is congruent with the routine activities idea of increasing the number of intimate handlers of potential offenders (Felson, 1986). Crime opportunity theories try to explain the etiology of crime events rather than explaining the motivations of criminal offenders. This focus on understanding the underlying situations and dynamics that cause crime events to recur rather than attempting to diagnose individual criminal dispositions leads to a very practical crime prevention orientation that fits well with focused deterrence activities.

Finally, focused deterrence strategies have developed ways of bringing these resources and dynamics to bear on high-risk groups and individuals, sometimes in the particular moments that they are at highest risk. As noted, it is not particularly unusual for communities to undertake anti-violence activities, such as peace walks and youth programming. Typically, such activities are extremely diffuse: a peace walk may cross entire neighborhoods, and youth programming address, for example, young men age 18–24. The community capacity and informal social control represented by the walk may not be particularly meaningful when spread across entire neighborhoods; a fraction of that capacity, however, can be extremely meaningful when it is deployed in direct contact and communication with the handful of group members driving violence across those neighborhoods. Similarly, the impact of existing youth programming capacity can go up dramatically when a fraction of it is directed toward the highest-impact group member at the moment that they are most primed for violent retaliation.

4.4 Reducing Opportunities through Situational Crime Prevention

The growing situational crime prevention discipline has supported the development of problem-oriented policing since its inception in the United Kingdom's Home Office Research Unit during the early 1980s (Clarke & Mayhew, 1980). Rather than preventing crime by addressing large social conditions such as poverty and inequality, situational crime prevention seeks to modify local environments to reduce crime opportunities. As described by Ronald V. Clarke (1997: 6), situational crime prevention techniques consist of opportunity-reduction measures that are "(1) directed at highly specific forms of crime (2) that involve the management, design, or manipulation of the immediate environment in as systematic and permanent way as possible (3) so as to increase the effort and risks of crime and reduce the rewards as perceived by a wide range of offenders." An action research model guides the situational analysis of crime problems and methodically identifies underlying conditions that cause problems to persist, gives rise to alternative responses logically linked to these conditions, and assesses the results of implemented responses.

Problem-oriented policing, as envisioned by Herman Goldstein (1990), uses the same iterative process rooted in action research. As such, while the approaches developed separately, focused deterrence and situational crime prevention are considered crime control complements (Braga & Kennedy,

2012; Skubak Tillyer & Kennedy, 2008). At face value, many of the crime prevention elements of focused deterrence seem to be very traditional criminal justice approaches. However, linking these elements to situational crime prevention helps to delineate the new crime control ideas advanced by focused deterrence. Both approaches seek to change offender decision making. Here, we focus on the decisions made to commit a specific criminal act, such as shooting at rival gangs, rather than decisions to become involved in crime or to persist or desist in criminal offending (Cornish & Clarke, 2003). The links between focused deterrence and situational crime prevention are identified for the key areas of increasing the effort, increasing risks, reducing rewards, reducing provocations, and removing excuses. It is important to note here that some of these opportunity-reducing measures focus on preventing crime at small high-risk crime places (or crime "hot spots") and build on a rigorous body of scientific evidence supporting place-based crime prevention policies and programs (e.g., see Weisburd, 2015; Braga, Turchan, et al., 2019).

4.4.1 Increasing Effort

Situational crime prevention attempts to increase the effort that criminals must make to complete a criminal act (Clarke, 1997). A varied set of particular interventions attempt to do so, such as target hardening, controlling access to facilities, screening exits, deflecting offenders, and controlling tools and weapons (Cornish & Clarke, 2003). Situational measures that increase offender effort to commit crimes can be included in focused deterrence interventions to develop a more robust response to the targeted behaviors of gangs, criminally active groups, and high-rate offenders. For instance, gang-involved youth not only offend at a higher rate when compared to nongang youth (Esbensen & Huizinga, 1993), but they also commit a wide range of crimes. GVI strategies can exploit the high-rate, varied offending patterns of targeted groups to develop a "thicker" response to their problem behaviors. This fuller approach can include changing the environments in which gangs congregate, commit offenses together, and launch plans to retaliate against their rivals. Controlling access to and screening exits from public housing and other facilities (apartment buildings, bars, etc.) could disrupt the ability of gangs to associate with each other. In turn, this could both impede group processes that facilitate violate and make it more difficult for rivals to find other gang members targeted for retaliatory shootings. Gangs often rely on illegal means to generate income; increasing the effort required to sell drugs at specific locations, commit burglaries and steal cars, and rob others could increase the deterrent power of a focused response by limiting illicit income opportunities.

A particularly interesting development within focused deterrence is the realization that the "guardians" so central to traditional situational crime prevention can themselves be offenders – who nonetheless can be brought to exercise powerful influences over other offenders. For instance, in Lowell, Massachusetts, the interagency working group recognized that they could systematically prevent street violence among Asian street gangs by targeting the gambling interests of older, influential members (Braga, Pierce, et al., 2008). When a street gang was violent, the Lowell police targeted the gambling businesses run by the older members of the gang. The enforcement activities ranged from serving a search warrant on the business that houses the illegal enterprise and making arrests to simply placing a patrol car in front of the suspected gambling location to deter gamblers from entering. The working group coupled these tactics with the delivery of a clear message, "when the gang kids associated with you act violently, we will shut down your gambling business. When violence erupts, no one makes money" (Braga et al., 2006: 40). These possibilities have led to the idea of deliberately mobilizing even serious offenders as "intimate handlers" of other offenders in ways consistent with increasing the effort required to commit crimes as well as other core situational crime prevention ideas (Skubak Tillyer & Kennedy, 2008).

4.4.2 Increasing Risk

Changing offender decisions about the risks they face when committing specific crimes is a core premise of both approaches. For instance, GVI focused deterrence attempts to increase the objective sanction risks by enhancing the intensity of enforcement focused on selected offenders while at the same time modifying their perceptions of apprehension risks by directly communicating this change to targeted groups and individuals. Ongoing intelligence analysis ensures that group members are not anonymous to partnering law enforcement agencies and continued offending is detected and immediately addressed. Triggering events, such as killing a rival gang member, provoke a swift and certain response by law enforcement agencies that is complemented by informal sanctions mobilized by community partners designed to weaken pro-offending norms. Criminal justice partners deliver varied sanctions that are customized to the crime dynamics associated with the offending group and to the specific criminal behaviors of specific individuals in the group. In addition to stopping immediate outbreaks of group violence, communications to rivals and allies of targeted groups seek to prevent further violence by increasing their perceived risks of apprehension and further weakening pro-offending norms and narrative in these extending co-offending networks (Braga, Apel, & Welsh, 2013; Braga et al., 2019).

More traditional situational measures are also implemented as part of the "pulling levers" work in focused deterrence strategies. The range and quality of the varying enforcement and regulatory levers that can be pulled on offending groups and key actors in criminal networks are powerfully enhanced by considering actions such as extending guardianship, assisting natural surveillance, strengthening formal surveillance, reducing anonymity of offenders, and mobilizing place managers (Braga & Kennedy, 2012; Skubak Tillyer & Kennedy, 2008). For instance, the Cincinnati Initiative to Reduce Violence, a GVI focused deterrence program, used civil forfeiture techniques to shut down a very disorderly bar that experienced persistent serious violence (Engel et al., 2010). Similarly, the High Point DMI used call-in sessions with landlords of drug houses to make certain that these place managers addressed persistent drug selling problems on their properties immediately to avoid swift and certain law enforcement and civil code violation penalties (Kennedy & Wong, 2009).

4.4.3 Reducing Rewards

In many cities suffering from high levels of gun violence, the majority of fatal and nonfatal shootings are generated by ongoing disputes among gangs and criminally active groups (Braga, Kennedy, & Tita, 2002). In these very violent environments, status is conferred on groups and individuals within these groups who are willing to behave violently (see, e.g., Anderson, 1999). The status rewards for violent behavior encourage further violence by promoting pro-offending norms and narratives within these high-risk social networks. Focused deterrence seeks to reverse this dynamic by attaching negative consequences to the same violent behavior that once increased the status of groups and individuals within street hierarchies. In essence, focused deterrence attempts to deny the benefits of violence by reversing this process of status accrual: where before violence brought respect, it instead represents increased official attention and the violation of clear community norms and standards.

Focused deterrence programs use other approaches to deny the benefits of crime accrued by offending groups and individual offenders (Skubak Tillyer & Kennedy, 2008). One such benefit-denying situational measure involves removing targets. For instance, interagency working groups have reduced the presence of gang members who are targeted for retaliatory shootings in high-risk places and at high-risk times by enhancing the conditions and increasing monitoring of offenders under probation and parole supervision, and by mobilizing the community through actions such as peace walks through gang turfs (Braga & Kennedy, 2012). Limiting group and individual profits from criminal behavior is an obvious form of reward reduction. Shutting down drug markets can counter outbreaks of gun violence by denying the ability of group members to earn money. Rather than earning respect and status, group members who shoot rivals and subsequently bring enforcement attention on their illicit sources of income would be subjected to anger and disassociation from the group.

4.4.4 Reducing Provocation

As described earlier, the communications of anti-violence messages are explicitly designed to exploit group dynamics that drive many crime problems. Sanction risks are communicated internally within groups from offenders who directly received the message via call-ins, custom notifications, and street conversations with authorities to other group members. Credible enforcement actions and persistent surveillance by law enforcement agencies can influence the rationality of group members to stop encouraging violent norms that lead to outbreaks of shootings (Skubak Tillyer & Kennedy, 2008). Citywide communications of the deterrence message, supported by concrete examples of enforcement actions delivered to groups that did not obey the rules, undermine the pro-violence norms as group members realize that their rivals are operating under the same rules as they are.

The idea of reducing group provocations to commit violence developed as the Boston Gun Project proceeded. Working group members hypothesized that a meaningful spell of dramatically decreased youth violence may serve as a "firebreak" that caused a much longer period of reduced youth violence in the future (Kennedy, Piehl, & Braga, 1996). The belief was that Boston youth violence had become a self-sustaining cycle involving a very small number of youth with objectively high levels of victimization risks that led to self-protective behaviors such as illegal gun acquisition and use, gang formation, and tough "street" behavior; these behaviors then became another input into the existing cycle of violence. If this violent cycle could be halted, a new equilibrium might be established at a much lower level of risk for these youth, perhaps without the need for continued criminal justice and social service intervention. An effective gang violence reduction intervention with meaningful short-term impacts on group provocations could have a disproportionate, sustainable long-term effect on group violence.

4.4.5 Removing Excuses

Community-based responses in focused deterrence assisted the removal of excuses used by offenders to justify their continued criminal behavior. During call-ins and through street conversations, community members challenge the norms and narratives perpetuated by targeted offenders that suggest racism, poverty, and injustice serve as valid excuses for their continued violent behavior. For instance, in Boston, activist black clergy invalidate these excuses by telling gang members that racism, poverty, and injustice did not justify their decisions to shoot and kill other young people who experienced the same social disadvantages (Winship & Berrien, 1999; Braga, Turchan, & Winship, 2019). Community partners also collaborated with law enforcement and social service agencies to set the "don't shoot" rules for gangs and criminally active groups and sought to alert the conscience of these individuals by appealing to inherent moral values against taking lives, harming their neighborhoods, and hurting their mothers by being killed or incarcerated at a location far away for a very long time. Beyond serving as an independent good, the availability of social services in focused deterrence programs also helps to invalidate excuses used by offenders by providing alternatives, such as employment and other opportunities, to their continued criminality (Braga & Kennedy, 2012).

Situational crime prevention also attempts to decrease crime by facilitating offender compliance with laws and rules. Focused deterrence strategies similarly try to make it easier for offenders to follow rules. However, they do so in very specific ways. Many gang members do not want to behave in the violent ways required by street honor codes but are under strong peer pressure to do so. The deterrence regime imposed on gangs makes it easier for individuals to back away from pro-violence norms, as the very real risk of punishment for all group members undermines the street honor code. Enhancing community norms against violence facilitates resistance against internal and external pressure to behave violently. In the seminal Boston Ceasefire experience, this was framed as an "honorable exit" from serious violence as a result of modified objective punishment risks and group dynamics (Kennedy, Braga, & Piehl, 2001). In essence, gang members were able to comply with the law and rules set by the Ceasefire working group (and adhere to their own personal values against hurting others) without drawing negative attention from their peers for not behaving in "expected" violent ways.

5 Ensuring Proper Implementation of Focused Deterrence Strategies

A growing body of rigorous evaluation evidence shows that focused deterrence strategies generate significant crime reduction impacts when applied to gang and group-related violence, disorderly street drug markets, and repeat offender problems (Braga, Weisburd, & Turchan, 2018; Weisburd & Majmundar, 2018). Focused deterrence strategies also seem to be very promising as a mechanism to improve strained relationships between minority neighborhoods and the police departments that serve them through the principled engagement of community members, engagement of offenders in procedurally-just offender notification sessions, provision of services and opportunities to offenders (Brunson, 2015; Meares, 2009). Nevertheless, these benefits can only be produced when these strategies are implemented properly. The available program evaluation evidence suggests that it can be difficult for local jurisdictions to achieve successful program implementations that remain robust over time (Kennedy, 2011; Braga, 2012). Worse, the deficient implementation of these interventions could exacerbate poor police-community relations and generate collateral harms through increased surveillance and harsh enforcement if these strategies are not appropriately focused (Griffiths & Christian, 2015). Such issues with fidelity seem to be emerging in certain European interventions informed by focused deterrence but not in fact adhering to its fundamental principles (Rowe & Søgaard, 2020).

Focused deterrence interventions are comprised of multifaceted activities and a complex interagency structure that presents multiple opportunities for implementation and fidelity problems. The systematic review of focused deterrence programs found that nearly one-third of the twenty-four included evaluations reported at least one threat to the treatment integrity stemming from implementation challenges (Braga, Weisburd, & Turchan, 2018). Implementation problems were found in GVI, DMI, and individual offender programs alike. For instance, the original Boston Ceasefire GVI program was discontinued despite several years of noteworthy success in reducing gang violence (Braga, Hureau, & Winship, 2008). Key challenges in sustaining the Boston Ceasefire intervention stemmed from a lack of ongoing analysis of evolving gun violence problems, inadequate governance structures that didn't support continued implementation after key working group members moved on to other positions, and political in-fighting in lead partnering agencies. Moreover, replication programs in Baltimore, Minneapolis, and San Francisco unraveled rapidly due to serious political problems and a lack of true interagency partnership after encouraging initial crime control success (see Kennedy, 2011; Braga, Turchan, & Winship, 2019). Other GVI programs also experienced very concerning program management challenges during implementation. The robustness of the Rochester Ceasefire intervention was limited by uncertain enforcement actions, poor interagency communication and coordination, and deficiencies in marketing the deterrence message to the targeted audience (Delaney, 2006). The Kansas City No Violence Alliance group violence reduction strategy had to overcome early problems stemming from a lack of leadership and poor communication among participating agencies before the intervention took hold (Fox, Novak, & Yaghoub, 2015).

The initial success of the Chicago PSN individual focused deterrence program spurred the aggressive expansion of the intervention to 24 percent of the city's police districts. Increased resources did not accompany the expansion and the resulting program was not well coordinated or supported in the additional areas.

Not surprisingly, the expanded PSN effort was not associated with any discernible crime control gains in the treated areas relative to comparison areas (Grunwald & Papachristos, 2017). After the demonstrated success of the DMI focused deterrence approach in High Point and elsewhere, the U.S. Bureau of Justice Assistance (BJA) funded an effort to systematically replicate the strategy in thirty-two sites around the United States (Saunders, Robbins, & Ober, 2017). Only seven of the thirty-two sites implemented a program with enough integrity to warrant a formal evaluation. However, the RAND Corporation evaluation noted that these seven sites experienced difficulty implementing the DMI program properly. Deficiencies ranged from a lack of support from partnering agencies and community groups to uncertain identification of key players in targeted drug markets to diminished follow-up on enforcement and social service promises after completed call-ins with drug offenders; notably, the BJA approach greatly diminished or entirely eliminated the racial reconciliation focus that is central to DMI (Saunders et al., 2016). Two of the seven sites failed to make it past the planning phase of the intervention while only four sites conducted at least one call-in and completed all five phases. The BJA-supported evaluation of these seven sites found that DMI programs with greater implementation fidelity experienced the largest reductions in crime (Saunders, Robbins, & Ober, 2017). As described earlier, the systematic review attributed the smaller effect sizes observed for DMI programs to compromises in the treatment as delivered in the included program evaluations (Braga, Weisburd, & Turchan, 2018).

As more cities have included focused deterrence as a central element of their broader approach to reduce crime, systematic efforts have been launched to ensure proper program implementation. Most prominently, the NNSC has developed a range of practitioner-friendly guides to structure program activities and promote the integrity of focused deterrence strategies. For example, the NNSC (2016) suggests that after a call-in is completed:

1. The working group should meet to recap the call-in and plan future project activities.
2. Data analysis should be ongoing and performance metrics continuously tracked.
3. Follow-through on promises made at call-ins must materialize (e.g., enforcement actions, connecting clients to social services, and continuing to engage with the moral voices of the community).
4. Communication with clients should be ongoing via holding additional call-ins, conducting custom notifications at the residences of clients, contacting high-risk individuals not under community supervision, and interrupting escalating violence.

We highly encourage interested readers to consult the various resources available through the NNSC that aid local jurisdictions in maintaining and ensuring treatment integrity from the outset of implementation.[3]

Beyond these resources on specific programmatic activities and strategic orientation, cities need to develop the following capabilities to facilitate the successful implementation of focused deterrence: creating a network of capacity, developing accountability structures and sustainability plans, and conducting upfront and ongoing problem analysis.

5.1 Creating a Network of Capacity

Convening an interagency working group with a locus of responsibility for managing the targeted crime problem is a key operational component of focused deterrence (Braga, Kennedy, & Tita, 2002). The working group needs to be supported by a larger collaboration that spans the boundaries that divide criminal justice agencies from one another, criminal justice agencies from human service agencies, and criminal justice agencies from the community. These kinds of collaborations are necessary to legitimize, fund, equip, and operate complex strategies that are most likely to succeed in both controlling and preventing equally complicated problems such as serious youth violence (Moore, 2002). In Boston, an existing network was well positioned to launch the highly effective Operation Ceasefire gang violence reduction strategy because criminal justice agencies, community groups, and social service agencies coordinated and combined their efforts in ways that could magnify their separate effects (Braga, Turchan, & Winship, 2019). Ceasefire capitalized on these existing relationships by focusing the network on the problem of serious gang violence.

Focused deterrence strategies strive to launch "relationship intensive" interventions rooted in trust, mutual accountability, and the capacity of a diverse set of individuals to work together toward a common goal. Delivering robust response to complicated crime problems, such as gang violence, requires effective collaborations. Unfortunately, the fact that such collaborations are needed does not guarantee that they inevitably emerge or, once developed, that they are sustained. There are many significant obstacles to their development and maintenance such as giving up control over scarce resources that could compromise agencies' traditional missions, aligning agencies' individual work efforts into a functional enterprise, and developing a collective leadership among a group of individuals aligned with the needs of their individual organizations (Bardach, 1998). Prior to the launch of any working group, jurisdictions need to identify and address these

---

[3] https://nnscommunities.org/ (accessed January 2, 2020).

obstacles, or the resulting focused deterrence intervention will not be implemented properly.

Overcoming distrust problems is a focal concern when jurisdictions attempt to create and manage effective capacity-building collaborations (Bardach, 1998). Distrust destroys the creative process that criminal justice agencies and community-based organizations are necessarily engaged in when developing multifaceted responses to complex crime problems. As elsewhere, distrust characterized the relationship among criminal justice organizations and between criminal justice organizations and the minority community in Boston (Braga, Turchan, & Winship, 2019). As they struggled to halt the epidemic of youth violence in the early 1990s, criminal justice practitioners and community members in Boston were able to overcome their historical distrust and form productive working relationships.

Trust was built as the divergent Boston stakeholder groups developed a common understanding of the nature of the youth violence problem (i.e., it was primarily driven by ongoing disputes amongst criminally active offenders involved in gangs) and by experimenting with new partnerships and programs such as police-probation partnerships to ensure gang-involved probationers were abiding by the conditions of their community supervision, police collaborations with street outreach workers to facilitate truces between warring gang factions, and investigations of the sources of illegal guns to gangs through federal, state, and local law enforcement enterprises (Kennedy, Piehl, & Braga, 1996). While these initiatives did not produce meaningful impacts on youth violence, the trusting relationships and innovative practices served as important inputs into the working group process and served as the foundation on which the Ceasefire initiative was built. Of course, working groups can be forced together and, sometimes, can implement short-term programs that have promising initial results. However, if the initiative is not based on a shared understanding of the problem and cemented through functional partnerships, the initiative will fall apart.

5.2 Developing Accountability Structures and Sustainability Plans

The reliance of focused deterrence programs on a small number of key actors across multiple organizations to implement the strategy successfully can make these initiatives highly vulnerable to personnel turnover. Unless there are strong accountability structures and sustainability plans in place, loss of key personnel can disrupt working group processes and hinder the preventive actions available through the larger network of capacity. The continuity of the original Boston Ceasefire intervention was seriously damaged by personnel turnover among key criminal justice managers and important community stakeholders involved in the process (Braga, Hureau, & Winship, 2008). Fortunately, the consequences of personnel turnover can be minimized through *a priori* planning for these inevitable events. For instance, in response to substantial turnover of key staff involved with the Chicago PSN program, project coordinators conducted "reboot" trainings with new replacement staff to ensure buy-in and maintain treatment integrity (Grunwald & Papachristos, 2017).

The NNSC (2016) outlined two ways that program sustainability and accountability could be enhanced: (1) establishing a governing structure that extends beyond the working group and (2) creating a performance maintenance system for key activities as well as continually keeping partners engaged in the project. The Cincinnati Initiative to Reduce Violence (CIRV) developed a comprehensive approach to remedy sustainability concerns by the establishment of a formal multilevel governance structure. Prior to the start of the GVI program, CIRV staff recruited local business executives and social science researchers to contribute to the planning process by providing policy advice intended to enhance long-term viability of the intervention (Skubak Tillyer, Engel, & Lovins, 2012). These external experts assisted with the overall CIRV design in three key areas: "(a) development of an organizational structure, (b) utilization of corporate strategic planning principles for managing the work, and (c) systematic data collection to assist in decision making and outcome evaluation" (Skubak Tillyer, Engel, & Lovins, 2012: 978).

CIRV organizational structure designed by the outside experts comprised three tiers of program stakeholders (Engel, Tillyer, & Corsaro, 2013). The *governing board* was at the highest level and consisted of high ranking city officials who were responsible for overseeing the project, providing resources, and overcoming implementation obstacles. A *strategy and implementation team* reported to the governing board and included spokespersons, heads of individual strategy teams, consultants, and an executive director; this body was responsible for daily operations, strategy development, and monitoring results. Four *individual strategy teams*, including a law enforcement team, social services team, community engagement team, and systems team, were responsible for implementing specific components of the initiative. The governing board offered a stabilizing presence in the tiered organizational structure when personnel turnover among team leaders, consultants, and individual strategy team members occurred.

Outside experts contributed to the CIRV in a second area: incorporating corporate principles into project planning and implementation. The inclusion of corporate principles assisted project participants to organize, prioritize, and assign tasks needing to be accomplished. These assignments, along with related performance metrics, were tracked using "balanced scorecards" in order to promote accountability among teams for short-term performance assessments while also linking measures to overall strategy implementation (Skubak Tillyer, Engel, & Lovins, 2012: 980). There was initial resistance by participating law enforcement and social service providers to these oversight mechanisms. However, the value of the approach was confirmed when some team members experienced "mission creep" and the performance metrics served as a corrective influence realigning the work required to complete the assigned task with CIRV goals and objectives.

Systematic data collection was the third area where the external experts provided substantive implementation guidance to the CIRV. Establishing systematic data collection provided project managers and decision makers with the most thorough and accurate description of the serious violent crime problem possible. Beyond impact measures (e.g., the number of homicides or group-involved shootings), CIRV data collection efforts also incorporated several process measures intended to measure treatment fidelity. Process measures considered "the extent to which the message was delivered to the target population, the level of law enforcement action that was being taken against violent groups linked to a homicide, and details regarding the delivery of services to those who were requesting help" (Skubak Tillyer, Engel, & Lovins, 2012: 981–982). Other jurisdictions have also developed systematic data collection efforts to guide the implementation of focused deterrence. For instance, the Oakland Mayor's Office institutionalized their Ceasefire GVI program by establishing a directive designating that the initiative would be managed through weekly shooting reviews, biweekly coordination meetings, and bimonthly performance appraisals (Braga et al., 2019). As described in the next section, shooting reviews examined citywide shootings and violence dynamics by specific gangs to direct GVI intervention resources in efforts to prevent future incidents.

5.3 Conducting Upfront and Ongoing Problem Analyses

Jurisdictions looking to implement focused deterrence programs properly *must* conduct upfront and ongoing analyses of targeted crime problems. Simply adopting particular tactics implemented in other cities, like call-ins or partnerships with clergy, will not result in the development and implementation of an effective strategy. Partnering agencies in specific jurisdictions need to follow the process, which begins with an upfront analysis of the targeted crime problem. Problem analysis involves conducting in-depth, systematic analysis and assessment of crime problems (Goldstein, 1990). The role of problem analysis in focused deterrence, and problem-oriented policing more generally, is crucial as it requires the careful examination of underlying factors that lead to crime and disorder problems. Following the completion of the initial analysis, key elements of the focused deterrence framework can be customized to local crime conditions and the operational capacities of part-nering agencies.

Gangs, criminally active groups, and street-level drug markets are often focal concerns in focused deterrence projects. How these problems are understood is a critical factor in designing an effective response. While there are salient parallels in gang problems across jurisdictions, such as the limited participation of youth in gangs (Esbensen & Huizinga, 1993) and the expressive nature of much gang violence (Decker, 1996), the character of criminal and disorderly youth gangs and groups varies widely both within and across cities (Curry, Ball, & Fox, 1994). Similarly, while there are consistent patterns in drug consumption and distribution across cities, the factors of production for local drug markets – such as specific characteristics of venues, buyers' access to the venue and income, sellers' labor and operating scope within venues, and drug market participant perceptions of impunity (Kleiman & Young, 1995) – can also vary both within and across places (Weisburd & Green, 1995). The diversity and complexity of these crime and disorder problems places a premium on the quality of problem analysis in focused deterrence interventions.

Research and practical experience suggest that problem analysis, as per-formed in most localities, is generally shallow and unfortunately provides little insight into underlying conditions and dynamics that cause crime problems to persist (Braga & Weisburd, 2019). As such, the resultant crime prevention responses, whether in a problem-oriented policing process or focused deter-rence framework, tend to rely upon traditional or faddish responses rather than engaging a broad search for customized responses. In successful focused deterrence projects, problem analysis work benefited considerably from strong working partnerships between criminal justice agencies and academic institu-tions (e.g., see Kennedy, Braga, & Piehl, 1996; Tita et al., 2004; Engel et al., 2010). In these projects, academic researchers provide "real-time social sci-ence" aimed at refining the interagency working group's understanding of gang violence, creating information products for both strategic and tactical use, testing – often in elementary, but important, fashion – prospective intervention ideas, and maintaining a focus on outcomes and the evaluation of performance (Braga, Kennedy, & Tita, 2002: 284).

The problem analysis research need not employ sophisticated methodo-logical approaches. The goal of the work is to identify key issues in the etiology of targeted crime problems – for instance, determining who is killing whom and the role that gangs and criminally active groups might play in driving recurring violence – so working groups can customize core focused deterrence elements to the nature of their problem and articulate the logic of the intervention to participating agencies and the public. Research techniques can include straightforward crime incident reviews and group audits where academics draw on the experiential assets of knowledgeable practitioners to develop detailed qualitative and quantitative insights on the nature of crime events and the criminally active groups and gangs that perpetrate these incidents (Klofas & Hipple, 2006). More sophisticated crime mapping and social network analysis techniques are also used to understand the spatial distribution of gang turfs and drug markets and the criminogenic relationships amongst co-offenders in rival and allied gangs and criminally active groups (Kennedy, Braga, & Piehl, 1997; McGloin, 2005).

Social network analyses, in particular, have been very helpful in both designing focused deterrence interventions based on the upfront analysis work on the nature of targeted crime problems and managing the intervention through the ongoing analysis of conflicts and alliances amongst connected groups. For instance, conflicts amongst Cape Verdean gangs were a prominent feature of a resurgence of Boston gang violence in the mid-2000s (Braga, Hureau, & Winship, 2008). Social network analysis revealed that 85 percent of total shootings in a Cape Verdean neighborhood were concentrated amongst a co-offending network of 763 individuals connected to ten gangs who represented less than 3 percent of the resident population of that neighborhood (Figure 8); what is more, each "handshake" an individual was closer to a gunshot victim in the network increased their personal risk of gunshot injury by 25 percent (Papachristos, Braga, & Hureau, 2012). In Oakland, continued social network analyses of gang conflicts and alliances were used to guide Ceasefire/GVI communications and reduce gun offending by gangs not subject to enforcement but socially connected to gangs that had been so subjected (Figure 9; Braga et al., 2019). This area is developing rapidly in focused deterrence theory and practice (Wheeler et al., 2019).

"Shooting scorecards" greatly aid the implementation of GVI programs, especially when supported by a management accountability system, by helping to ensure that the groups most active in gun violence, and the groups that offend after law enforcement has delivered the deterrence message during an intervention, receive the enforcement attention they merit and as much supportive and preventive intervention as possible (Braga, Hureau, & Grossman, 2014). Scorecards ensure that GVI partners stay focused on risky groups over time and support the implementation of the strategy as a whole. In essence, shooting scorecards create

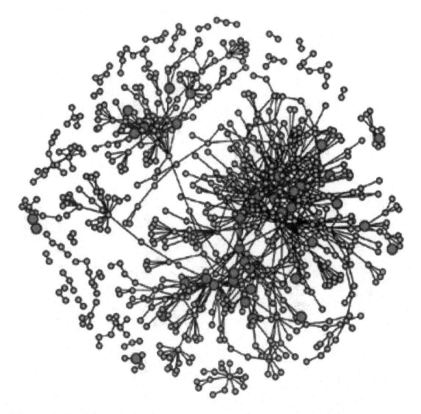

Figure 8. Social Networks of High-Risk Individuals in a Boston Community, 2008

Source: Papachristos, Braga and Hureau (2012: **998**).

Note: Smaller nodes represent individuals in the network. Larger nodes represent individuals in the network who suffered a fatal or nonfatal gunshot wound.

rank-ordered frequencies of the criminal groups that commit the highest number of shootings and experience the greatest number of shooting victimizations during a specific time period (such as a week, month, or year). Law enforcement uses the data to identify the most violent groups, and these groups receive systematic consideration for focused deterrence interventions. Using scorecards, police departments can more easily understand the share of gun violence generated by ongoing disputes between rival gangs, internal gang conflicts, drug market violence, personal disputes, robberies, and other street dynamics. Police departments can then track and monitor gun violence trends at the group level over time.

Figure 10 presents an example of a shooting scorecard used by the Boston Police Department in 2010. It shows that the number of shootings committed by the CVO / Homes Avenue, H-Block, Orchard Park, Greenwood, Lenox,

Direct and Vicarious Ceasefire Treatment Applied to Oakland Gangs

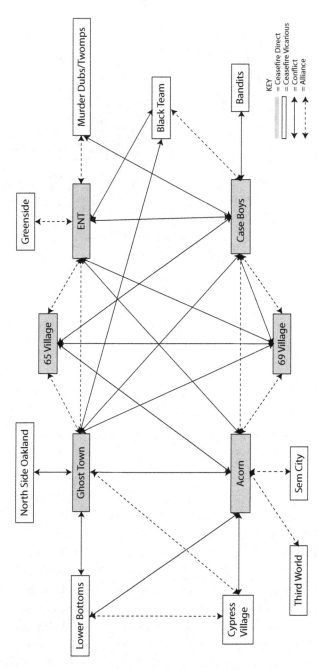

Figure 9. Direct and Vicarious Ceasefire Treatment Applied to Oakland Gangs.

Source: Braga et al. (2019: 543).

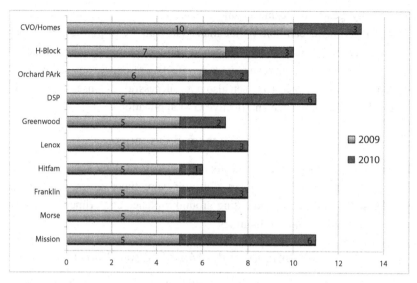

Figure 10. Number of Shootings the 2009 Most Frequent Boston Shooter
Gangs Committed in 2010.

Source: Braga, Hureau, & Grossman (2014: 23).

Hitfam, Morse, and Franklin Field gangs decreased between 2009 and 2010. While any implemented violence intervention clearly warrants more careful evaluation, this simple year-to-year comparison suggests that shootings committed by these gangs were in short-term decline. In contrast, shootings by the DSP and Mission gangs increased between 2009 and 2010. This suggests that the Boston Police needed to reassess existing violence interventions focused on these groups; alternatively, if they weren't focusing violence interventions directly on these groups, they needed to implement a strategic response immediately.

The uses of shooting scorecards are consistent with the police performance management ideals of Compstat (Heinrich & Braga, 2010). While it has many features, Compstat can be generally viewed as a combined technical and managerial system that embeds the technical system for the collection and distribution of police performance data in a broader managerial system (Silverman, 1999; McDonald, 2002). This system is designed to focus the organization on specific objectives, usually involving crime reduction, by holding a subset of managers accountable for using organizational resources appropriately in pursuit of these objectives (Moore & Braga, 2003). Shooting scorecards can be incorporated into Compstat-like processes to ensure that police departments appropriately focus scarce resources on the groups that consistently generate the most gun violence (Braga, Hureau, & Grossman, 2014). Departments can hold police managers who are responsible for group violence prevention accountable for generating the desired violence reduction impacts. These departments can reassess ineffective responses and launch more appropriate interventions. They can also note successful responses and contribute to a body of knowledge on effective GVI applications.

6 Policy, Practice, and Discourse

Beyond these defined aspects and impacts of focused deterrence theory and practice, the approach has been part of driving, sometimes centrally, important broader shifts in thinking and acting around violence and crime, preventing violence and crime, and communities.

6.1 Small Numbers of the Most Serious Offenders

Perhaps no more important fundamental shift in, especially, American policing over the last decades is the now widespread understanding that the most serious violence and crime problems are driven by very small numbers of extremely active and high-risk people. At the time focused deterrence was first being developed, for example, the most dominant idea in U.S. crime policy was that of "superpredators" described as "fatherless, Godless, and jobless" young men, "radically impulsive, brutally remorseless youngsters," (Bennett, DiIulio, and Walters, 1996: 79, 27) "coming at us in waves over the next two decades" (DiIulio, 1996: 14). Academic and popular ideas of fundamentally deviant communities governed by a "culture of violence" were widespread. Stark (1993: 486) cited Princeton professor Cornel West's assessment of a black youth underclass embodying a "'walking nihilism' of drug addiction, alcoholism, homicide, and suicide"; Harvard psychiatrist Alvin Puissant's diagnosis of a black "subculture of violence" driven by self-hatred; and Washington, DC congressional delegate Eleanor Holmes Norton's characterization of "a complicated, predatory ghetto subculture."

Such ideas fueled widespread notions of, especially, black neighborhoods as dangerous places full of dangerous people and provided fertile ground for destructive legislation (Johnson, 2014) and intrusive, indiscriminate policing strategies. New York City pursued a "zero tolerance" approach – widely viewed as in direct competition with focused deterrence (Butterfield, 2000) – with tremendous national and international influence. Former New York City Mayor Michael Bloomberg said in 2015 that crime had gone down in the city "because we put all the cops in minority neighborhoods. Why do we do it? Because that's where all the crime is, . . . and the way you get the guns out of the kids' hands is to throw them up against the wall and frisk them" (Jacobs, Campanile, & Golding, 2020). At its peak in 2011, the New York City Police Department (NYPD) made almost 700,000 stops a year, overwhelmingly of young men in minority neighborhoods.[4]

In contrast, the NYPD now pursues an approach it calls "precision policing," based on the idea, as put by then-NYPD commissioner William Bratton in 2018, that police should pay careful attention to "the few who make communities unsafe" (Bratton & Anderson, 2018). "We know that there are very few people involved in the violence and crime in New York City," said Bratton's successor, former Commissioner James O'Neill (Loughlin, 2016), an understanding now routinely heard in policing and, increasingly, elsewhere. There are a number of drivers of this profound shift, including especially a growing body of scholarship based on social network analysis (McGloin, 2005), but it has perhaps been most centrally established by the now-decades of police exposure to the logic and practice of focused deterrence and, in particular, GVI. As the mayor, city manager, and police chief of Cincinnati, Ohio, wrote after more than a decade of implementing GVI, "By focusing on repeat violent offenses rather than high-volume misdemeanors, Cincinnati police have reduced the violence, reduced the sense that African American communities are 'over-policed,' and have increased public trust in law enforcement" (Cranley, Duhaney, & Isaac, 2020).

In city after city, GVI initiatives have shown the central fact of extraordinary concentration of homicide offending and victimization; police and political leadership and the public have been exposed to that fact; and police, especially, have heard from their peers and outside experts at decades of conferences, conventions, trainings, and the like. The notion has fundamentally taken hold and has shifted the thinking and practice of American policing. The NYPD, for example, has adopted GVI and makes wide additional use of custom notifications, which have come to be known internally as "no retals," for "no retaliation." A wide range of such changes in policy and practice driven by the – correct – idea that there are very few dangerous people in New York City brought the number of stops down 98 percent by 2017, while crime continued to fall. The shift in mainstream thinking this has fostered is difficult to exaggerate; in 2016, the tabloid *New York Daily News*,[5] for example, published an editorial frankly admitting, "We were wrong: Ending stop and frisk did not end stopping crime," and crediting NYPD's "knowing whom to target, when and where."

---

[4] www.nyclu.org/en/stop-and-frisk-data (accessed February 16, 2020).

[5] www.nydailynews.com/opinion/wrong-ending-stop-frisk-not-stopping-crime-article-1.2740157 (Accessed on February 16, 2020.)

6.2 The Overlap of Offending and Victimization

Closely linked is the way in which especially, again, GVI has brought home the fact – again long established in scholarly literature, but not taken on board in criminal justice and other thinking and practice – that offenders and victims are very often the same people. GVI's focus on small pools of extremely high-risk people has brought the idea into the fore of attention for police and others. GVI research has invariably shown the concentration of both offending and victimization in cities' small populations of groups; implementations have highlighted it further as, for example, group members identified a week or two before call-ins don't make it because they have been killed in the interim. It is now not unusual in policing to hear attention to violent offenders' direct exposure to family violence, direct and vicarious exposure to community violence, and the role of risk and trauma in driving gun acquisition and use, "gang" formation, and the like: a sea change from not so very long ago.

6.3 "Groups" and Group Dynamics

Focused deterrence has brought to the forefront of crime and violence prevention the central role of groups and group dynamics. Well-established in multiple academic literatures (sociology and its branch criminology, anthropology, and social psychology, to name a few, are all predicated on the recognition of groups and group processes) and in scholarship about crime via core findings about gangs, co-offending, and networks, these ideas had stubbornly resisted practical application. The main culprit here was the formal and popular understandings of "gang." While generations of gang scholarship have failed to come to any agreement on what a gang is, and legal definitions are woefully inadequate (Kennedy, 2009b), the popular idea is clear: gangs have leadership, are structured and purposeful, use violence in support of gang economic interests, deliberately recruit new members, and the like. Since most violent groups are not at all like this, and the world of crime and violence is generally parsed into a received ascending hierarchy of solo offenders, "gangs," and organized crime, the central role of groups in driving violence was both extremely obvious and essentially unrecognized.

Bringing it to the surface has advanced both scholarship (again with the important and similar contribution of social network analysis) and practice. Systematic attention to violence on the ground has shown the importance of group-related violence and of establishing meaningful definitions and under-standings of "group" and "group-related" with respect to both people and incidents. Understanding of intra- and intergroup dynamics has shown why group members can do terrible things without necessarily being terrible people, the role of noneconomic motives such as respect and retaliation in driving violence, and why enormous attention and resources devoted to addressing individuals fails to reach group dynamics and produce impact. Police, again especially, are in the forefront of taking in and building on these insights; it is now routine for police to articulate the significance and nature of groups. "'Investigators are tracking 39 groups in the city,' said Sgt. Jim Glick, who heads GVI,'" wrote Bradbury in the *Pittsburgh Post-Gazette*. "Police prefer the term 'group' because they feel it better reflects the loose organization and shifting allegiances they see here than the word 'gang'" (Bradbury, 2017).

6.4 Operationalizing Informal Social Control

It has long been the scholarly understanding that informal social control is greatly more powerful than formal social control. That understanding has generally been descriptive and causal, without being seen as practical: informal social control was seen as endogenous to, for example, collective efficacy, without any notion of how it might be altered, improved, or mobilized, particularly in any proximate ways. New criminological directions such as situational crime prevention, routine activities theory, and operational innovations such as third-party policing have gone some way toward addressing that lack, particularly with framings of, and of how to mobilize, "guardians" (see, e.g., Matthews, 2014). For the most part, however, police and other criminal justice agencies have relied on their own enforcement capacities, and government and community groups have relied on their own prevention activities, to address violence and crime.

Focused deterrence has elevated, alongside enforcement and prevention, the "moral voice of the community" and the place and power of informal social control. (One of the authors routinely asks rooms full of law enforcement officials to raise their hands if they were afraid of the police growing up; a few hands go up. When he asks who was afraid of their mothers, every hand goes up.) Agencies that have long been highly focused and sophisticated in, for example, conducting a drug investigation or designing and running a job placement program are increasingly recognizing that they can be equally deliberate about mobilizing informal social control. Men who have been assumed to "have no regard for human life" turn out to pay close attention to community mothers who have lost their children to homicide, and to older, wiser "original gangsters"; government and community actors can engineer such engagements. A state corrections official told one of the authors that a prison plagued by sexual misbehavior, as in inmates throwing semen at female corrections officers, no longer had the issue since responding to such instances by arranging conference calls between a corrections official, the inmate in question, and his mother. Agencies that conduct custom notifications, an increasingly common practice, report that in practice talking to a close family member or a girlfriend frequently seems even more effective than direct contact with the subject of the notification. An initiative that began in Boston, Massachusetts, mobilizes – with police and prosecutorial support – women who have been drawn into facilitating men's gun violence to intervene with other women who might be at risk of doing so, and to change vulnerable women's norms around gun trafficking and diversion.[6] Such deliberate mobilization of informal social control is coming to occupy a framing and operational place in practical thinking about violence and crime prevention, alongside more traditional and deeply grooved notions of enforcement and prevention.

6.5 Reframing Deterrence

Finally, focused deterrence has fundamentally reset understandings around deterrence as a theoretical idea and as it can be applied in practice. In scholarship, deterrence theory had come to be dominated by rarified economic thinking, such as this from Piliavin et al. (1986: 101):

> Consider the following formal statement of an actor's utility under conditions of risk:
>
> $$E(U) = (1–p) U(y) + p U(y–F),$$
>
> where E(U) is the actor's expected utility from a contemplated activity, P is the likelihood of being punished for the activity, Y is the anticipated returns (material or psychic) from the activity, and F is the anticipated penalty resulting if the actor is punished for the activity.
>
> According to the statement, if for a given person, the expected utility of an illegal (legal) act is greater than the expected utility of other alternatives, the person will engage in the illegal (legal) act.

and by ideas of "rationality" that left no room for the impulsivity, chaos, and even self-destruction that is of course a routine part of crime and violence. "Recent criminological theorizing has been dominated by rational choice explanations that overemphasize the extent to which offending is an independent, freely chosen action," wrote Wright and Decker (1997: 120). "The reality for many offenders is that crime commission has become so routinized that it emerges almost naturally in the course of their daily lives, often occurring without substantial planning or deliberation." On the practical side, police and many others on the front line in criminal justice had given up on deterrence entirely: they believed in enforcement and especially in incapacitation, but held

---

[6] Operation Lipstick, www.operationlipstick.org (accessed February 16, 2020).

out little hope that anything except standing next to a potential criminal would stop him from misbehavior, notions both encapsulated and reinforced by images of offenders as "scumbags," "mopes," and sociopathic or worse. And for everybody involved, deterrence had come to be identified entirely with the workings (or lack thereof) of the criminal justice system.

Both positions were fundamentally out of touch with the simple and profound notion that acts that are known to come with costs will be performed less often. Both positions – that deterrence requires sophisticated calculation, and that large numbers of people are incapable of thinking clearly about, and/or do not care about, consequences – are incompatible with the plain evidence of every-day life. People look both ways before they cross the street – it doesn't take much sophistication or calculation not to want to be hit by a car – and for the most part drunks and schizophrenics do so as well. Thinking about deterrence had become so mannered that it was nearly impossible to see it for what it is.

Focused deterrence, in its theory and practice, has reinforced the simple idea that costs matter; has moved the fact that knowledge of costs, and the communication of that knowledge, is an essential part of deterrence from a purely theoretical matter to a practical one; has opened up the role deterrence can play in preventing violence and crime to include a central focus on groups and group dynamics, rather than on individuals; has decoupled the theory and practice of deterrence from reliance on criminal justice case processing; has incorporated powerful aspects of informal social control; has elevated the place of legitimacy, and with it individual and collective experiences of history, race, and harm; has perhaps for the first time in practice broken the automatic policy and popular association of deterrence with severity; and has attached deterrence to other theoretical and practical frameworks such as problem-oriented policing, situational crime prevention, and routine activities theory. The plain fact, now well established and widely accepted, that offenders and potential offenders *do* respond has undercut notions that they are irrational, unreachable, self-destructive, have "no regard for human life," and other such canards. Deterrence, far from being a necessarily extreme – or worse – exercise of state power, can now be seen as an organizing principle for effective, supportive, respectful, and limited engagement.

7 Conclusion

Focused deterrence emerged from the need to address the American homicide and gun violence crisis of the mid-1990s, and the self-evident failure of then-existing and foreseeable measures to rise to that challenge. Both with respect to the situation on the ground and with respect to any new intervention, the research that ensued represented a return to basics: the asking of simple but fundamental questions, using simple but powerful methods, about the violence itself; and an inquiry, guided by the answers to those questions, into what might work, guided by simple but powerful questions about impact, capacity, law, and fairness. The first set of questions led to an understanding of an extraordinary concentration of violent offending and victimization, the location of that concentration in groups, its association with an equally extraordinary range of other offending by groups and group members, and its being driven less by individual conviction and group interests than by unspoken and even unwelcome group dynamics. The second set of questions led to an application of deterrence, one of the oldest, simplest, and most powerful ideas in violence and crime control and in what is now criminology.

The one was almost eerily matched to the other. If homicide and gun violence were not concentrated in groups that were committing prodigious numbers of other crimes, the newly focused deterrence would not have worked; but it was, and they were. If group members were not fundamentally rational, and their worst behavior not entirely to their taste and driven by factors that were powerful but relatively superficial, they would not have responded as directly and profoundly; but they were, it was, and they did. If deterrence were not a flexible and powerful idea, it could not have been adapted to violent groups and group dynamics, and applied in a major American city largely by a handful of line-level practitioners with only the resources they could command; but it was, it could, and they did. If high-crime communities did not fundamentally respect the law and desire safety, and if group members did not fundamentally respect their communities, the informal social control built into the new deterrence would not have worked; but they did, and it did.

As this Element has demonstrated, all of these findings and ideas were not only present in but were *core aspects* of central traditions of research in criminology and other social sciences. The origin and subsequent refinement of focused deterrence has essentially been a rediscovery of these core ideas and their rearrangement and redeployment in practical ways (Kennedy, 1997, 2008). Conducting action research in violence and crime prevention rapidly teaches one very clearly that those who know the social science typically have scholarly knowledge, methodological expertise, and time to think, but little knowledge of and less contact with the problems on the ground, while those who know the problems on the ground do not know the scholarship and methods, and have no time whatsoever to think (Kennedy, 2019). Combining them showed the power of both together (Kennedy, 2019).

In retrospect, it is not in any way surprising that the situation on the ground in Boston was eerily suited to the new deterrence approach, and *vice versa*: the situation on the ground was simply a special case of a broader reality researchers had been examining for generations, and the approach was simply a special case of a set of operational ideas that had been in theoretical and practical development for far longer. The problem was that most people making and debating public policy on the violence problem, in Boston and elsewhere, knew little or nothing about either the situation on the ground or the relevant literatures; those in Boston and elsewhere knew one or the other but not both, and were in no position either to fix that or to figure out what they might mean together. The Boston Gun Project was an occasion to rediscover, revisit, and reintegrate facts on the ground with long traditions of theory, research, and practice: a process that subsequent focused deterrence theory, research, and interventions have continued since.

That process has created a general violence and crime problem-oriented heuristic; a set of proven approaches to group violence, drug markets, and individual violent offenders; a substantial body of other interventions without, at least as yet, a robust evaluation record; and a set of associated, specialized research and operational tools. These include protocols for mixed-method problem analyses and more or less real-time violence and crime tracking; techniques for communicating with high-risk groups and individuals; techniques for utilizing existing legal sanctions in new ways; techniques for mobilizing sanctions not associated with the criminal law; techniques for identifying and mobilizing sources of informal social control; a portfolio of facilitative, supportive measures; approaches to incorporating procedural justice and other methods intended to enhance legitimacy; and approaches to managing, assessing, and evaluating interventions. One way of characterizing the evolution of focused deterrence is that this roster has not changed much since the first framing of Operation Ceasefire in Boston twenty-five years ago – each of these elements was present then – while the way each of them is now conceived and implemented has changed dramatically. That can be expected to continue going forward; the way each of these elements is conceived and implemented likely will not look – and perhaps should not look – the same five, ten, and twenty-five years from now. So, very likely, will be the range of substantive problems known to be susceptible to focused deterrence intervention; that roster has also grown over time, and one hopes that that too will continue.

Several areas stand out as needing particular evaluation attention. For GVI focused deterrence interventions, there is now strong evidence of impact. However, additional rigorous evaluations of DMI and individual offender programs are needed. While more, and methodologically stronger, evaluations are always welcome, Roman, Forney, et al. (2019: 3) argue that "scholars and practitioners need evaluations designed to elucidate the critical components of these programs – results that show the theory of change accurately represents the change mechanisms at work on the ground." Within that set of components and processes, it seems particularly important to understand the links between attempts to enhance legitimacy; any actual changes in legitimacy; and any changes in voluntary compliance, police/community cooperation, and levels of violence and crime. There have been very few studies that explicitly examine whether and how focused deterrence creates legitimacy and procedural justice. This is a priority area for future research. It also seems important to sort out the workings and any contribution (or lack thereof) of informal social control; the provision of supportive services; changes in intra- and intergroup dynamics; and any impact focused deterrence has on reducing the exercise of the criminal law and, especially, arrest and incarceration. Within that set of now-proved focused deterrence interventions, there is need for evaluation of their implementation outside of the United States, which has the most experience with the strategies. Outside of it, there is need for evaluation of interventions directed at new substantive problems: some of them in implementation now, and others no doubt to be developed.

All of that is now entirely within the realm of the possible. Twenty-five years ago, the authors were part of a small team of practitioners and researchers desperate about violence in the United States, and in Boston in particular. That team fielded an intervention not even they were confident would work. It did; that basic intervention, and beyond that its implications and continued development, have created a body of theory and practice that has produced a bounded but meaningful body of effective applied work, and the potential for a good deal more. We can be optimistic that those implications and that continued development will continue to bear fruit.

References

Abt, T. (2019). *Bleeding Out: The Devastating Consequences of Urban Violence and a Bold New Plan for Peace in the Streets*, New York: Basic Books.

Abt, T. & Winship, C. (2016). *What Works in Reducing Community Violence*, Washington, DC: United States Agency for International Development.

Anderson, E. (1999). *Code of the Street: Decency, Violence and the Moral Life of the Inner City*, New York: Norton.

Bachman, R., Paternoster, R., & Ward, S. (1992). The rationality of sexual offending: Testing a deterrence/rational choice conception of sexual assault. *Law & Society Review*, 26 (2), 343–372.

Bardach, E. (1998). *Getting Agencies to Work Together*, Washington, DC: Brookings Institution Press.

Beccaria, C. (1764/1872). *On Crimes and Punishment*, Albany, NY: W.C. Little & Co.

Beetham, D. (1991). *The Legitimation of Power*, Atlantic Highlands, NJ: Humanities Press International.

Bell, M. (2016). Situational trust: How disadvantaged mothers reconceive legal cynicism. *Law & Society Review*, 50(2),314–347.

Bell, M. (2017). Police reform and the dismantling of legal estrangement. *Yale Law Journal*, 126 (7), 2054–2150.

Bennett, W., DiIulio, J., & Walters, J. (1996) *Body Count: Moral Poverty – And How to Win America's War Against Crime and Drugs*, New York: Simon & Schuster.

Bentham, J. (1789/1988). *The Principles of Morals and Legislation*, Amherst, NY: Prometheus Books.

Block, C.R. & Block, R. (1993). *Street Gang Crime in Chicago*. Washington, DC: National Institute of Justice, US Department of Justice.

Borges, D., Emiliano Rojido, E., & Cano, I. (2019). Avaliação de impacto do pacto Pelotas pela paz. Rio de Janeiro, Brazil: Laboratório de Análise da Violência, Universidade do Estado do Rio de Janeiro.

Bottoms, A., & Tankebe, J. (2012). Beyond procedural justice: A dialogic approach to legitimacy in criminal justice. *Journal of Criminal Law and Criminology*, 102 (1), 119–170.

Bradbury, S. (2017) City revives effort to quell gun violence by aggressively targeting gang members. *Pittsburgh Post-Gazette*, Aug. 7. www.post-gazette .com/local/city/2017/08/07/Pittsburgh-Police-gun-violence-gangs-group-intervention-David-Kennedy-PIRC/stories/201708070007

Boyle, D., Lanterman, J., Pascarella, J., & Cheng, C. (2010). The impact of Newark's Operation Ceasefire on trauma center gunshot wound admissions. *Justice Research and Policy*, 12 (2), 105–123.

Braga, A. (2003). Serious youth gun offenders and the epidemic of youth violence in Boston. *Journal of Quantitative Criminology*, 19 (1), 33–54.

Braga, A. (2004). *Gun Violence Among Serious Young Offenders*, num 23 of problem-oriented guides for police series, Washington, DC: US Department of Justice, Office of Community Oriented Policing Services.

Braga, A. (2008a). *Problem-Oriented Policing and Crime Prevention*, 2nd edn, Boulder, CO: Lynne Rienner Publishers.

Braga, A. (2008b). Pulling levers focused deterrence strategies and the prevention of gun homicide. *Journal of Criminal Justice*, 36 (4), 332–343.

Braga, A. (2012). Getting deterrence right? Evaluation evidence and complementary crime control mechanisms. *Criminology & Public Policy*, 11 (2), 201–210.

Braga, A., Apel, R., & Welsh, B. (2013). The spillover effects of focused deterrence on gang violence. *Evaluation Review*, 37 (3–4), 314–342.

Braga, A., Brunson, R., & Drakulich. K. (2019). Race, place, and effective policing. *Annual Review of Sociology*, 45, 535–555.

Braga, A., Hureau, D., & Grossman, L. (2014). *Managing the Group Violence Intervention: Using Shooting Scorecards to Track Group Violence*, Washington, DC: US Department of Justice, Office of Community Oriented Policing Services.

Braga, A., Hureau, D., & Papachristos, A. (2014). Deterring gang-involved gun violence: Measuring the impact of Boston's Operation Ceasefire on street gang behavior. *Journal of Quantitative Criminology*, 30 (1), 113–139.

Braga, A., Hureau, D., & Winship, C. (2008). Losing faith? Police, black churches, and the resurgence of youth violence in Boston. *Ohio State Journal of Criminal Law*, 6 (1), 141–172.

Braga, A. & Kennedy, D. (2012). Linking situational crime prevention and focused deterrence strategies. In N. Tilley and G. Farrell, eds., *The Reasoning Criminologist: Essays in Honour of Ronald V. Clarke*. London, UK: Taylor and Francis, pp. 51–65.

Braga, A., Kennedy, D., & Tita, G. (2002). New approaches to the strategic prevention of gang and group-involved violence. In C. R. Huff, ed., *Gangs in America*, 3rd edn. Thousand Oaks, CA: Sage Publications, pp. 271–286.

Braga, A., Kennedy, D., Waring, E., & Piehl, A. (2001). Problem-oriented policing, deterrence, and youth violence: An evaluation of Boston's Operation Ceasefire. *Journal of Research in Crime and Delinquency*, 38 (1), 195–225.

Braga, A., McDevitt, J., & Pierce, G. (2006). Understanding and preventing gang violence: Problem analysis and response development in Lowell, Massachusetts. *Police Quarterly*, 9 (1), 20–46.

Braga, A., Pierce, G., McDevitt, J., Bond, B., & Cronin, S. (2008). The strategic prevention of gun violence among gang-involved offenders. *Justice Quarterly*, 25 (1), 132–162.

Braga, A., Turchan, B., & Barao, L. (2019). The influence of investigative resources on homicide clearances. *Journal of Quantitative Criminology*, 35 (2), 337–364.

Braga, A., Turchan, B., Hureau, D., & Papachristos, A. (2019). Hot spots policing and crime reduction: An update of an ongoing systematic review and meta-analysis. *Journal of Experimental Criminology*, 15 (3), 289–311.

Braga, A., Turchan, B., & Winship, C. (2019). Partnership, accountability, and innovation: Clarifying Boston's experience with pulling levers. In D. Weisburd and A. Braga, eds., *Police Innovation: Contrasting Perspectives*, 2nd edn. New York: Cambridge University Press, pp. 227–250.

Braga, A., & Weisburd, D. (2012). The effects of focused deterrence strategies on crime: A systematic review and meta-analysis of the empirical evidence. *Journal of Research in Crime and Delinquency*, 49 (3), 323–358.

Braga, A., & Weisburd, D. (2012). Must we settle for less rigorous evaluations in large area-based crime prevention programs? Lessons from a Campbell review of focused deterrence. *Journal of Experimental Criminology*, 10 (4), 573–597.

Braga, A., & Weisburd, D. (2019). Problem-oriented policing: The disconnect between principles and practice. In D. Weisburd and A. Braga, eds., *Police Innovation: Contrasting Perspectives*, 2nd edn. New York: Cambridge University Press, pp. 182–204.

Braga, A., Weisburd, D., & Turchan, B. (2018). Focused deterrence strategies and crime control: An updated systematic review and meta-analysis of the empirical evidence. *Criminology & Public Policy*, 17 (1), 205–250.

Braga, A., Zimmerman, G., Barao, L., Farrell, C., Brunson, R., & Papachristos, A. (2019). Street gangs, gun violence, and focused deterrence: Comparing place-based and group-based evaluation methods to estimate direct and spillover deterrent effects. *Journal of Research in Crime and Delinquency*, 56 (4), 524–562.

Bratton, W., & Anderson, P. (2018). Precision policing. *City Journal*, www.city-journal.org/html/william-bratton-precision-policing-16084.html

Brunson, R. (2007). 'Police don't like black people': African American young men's accumulated police experiences. *Criminology & Public Policy*, 6 (1), 71–102.

Brunson, R. (2015). Focused deterrence and improved police-community relations: Unpacking the proverbial 'black box'. *Criminology & Public Policy*, 14 (3), 507–514.

Brunson, R., Braga, A., Hureau, D., & Pegram, K. (2015). We trust you, but not that much: Examining police–black clergy partnerships to reduce youth violence. *Justice Quarterly*, 32 (6), 1006–1036.

Bursik, R. & Grasmick, H. (1993). *Neighborhoods and Crime: The Dimensions of Effective Community Control*, Lexington, MA: Lexington Books.

Butterfield, F. (2000). Cities reduce crime and conflict without New York-style hardball. *New York Times*, www.nytimes.com/2000/03/04/nyregion/cities-reduce-crime-and-conflict-without-new-york-style-hardball.html

Chaiken, J., & Chaiken, M. (1982). *Varieties of Criminal Behavior*, Santa Monica, CA: RAND Corporation.

Circo, G., Krupa, J., McGarrell, E., & DeBiasi, A. (2019). The individual-level deterrent effect of "call-in" meetings on time to re-arrest. *Crime & Delinquency*, https://doi.org/10.1177/0011128719885869

Clark-Moorman, K., Rydberg, J., & McGarrell, E. (2019). Impact evaluation of a parolee-based focused deterrence program on community-level violence. *Criminal Justice Policy Review*, 30 (9), 1408–1430.

Clarke, R., ed. (1997). *Situational Crime Prevention: Successful Case Studies*, 2nd edn. Monsey, NY: Criminal Justice Press.

Clarke, R., & Weisburd, D. (1994). Diffusion of crime control benefits: Observations on the reverse of displacement. *Crime Prevention Studies*, 2, 165–184.

Cohen, J. (1988). *Statistical Power Analysis for the Behavioral Sciences*, 2nd edn. Hillsdale, NJ: Lawrence Erlbaum.

Cohen, L., & Felson, M. (1979). Social change and crime rate trends: A routine activity approach. *American Sociological Review*, 44 (4), 588–605.

Collins, J., Spencer, D., Snodgrass, J., &Wheeless, S. (1999). *Linkage of Domestic Violence and Substance Abuse Services*. Rockville, MD: National Criminal Justice Reference Service.

Cook, P. (1980). Research in criminal deterrence: Laying the groundwork for the second decade. In N. Morris and M. Tonry, eds., *Crime and Justice: An Annual Review of Research*, vol 2. Chicago: University of Chicago Press, pp. 211–268.

Cook, P. (2009). Robbery. In M. Tonry, ed., *The Oxford Handbook of Crime and Public Policy*. New York: Oxford University Press, pp. 102–114.

Cook, P., & Ludwig, J. (2006). Aiming for evidence-based gun policy. *Journal of Policy Analysis and Management*, 25(3), 691–735.

Cook, P., Ludwig, J., & Braga, A. (2005). Criminal records of homicide offenders. *Journal of the American Medical Association*, 294 (5), 598–601.

Cook, P., Ludwig, J., Venkatesh, S., & Braga, A. (2007). Underground gun markets. *The Economic Journal*, 117 (11), 558–588.

Cornish, D., & Clarke, R., eds. (1986). *The Reasoning Criminal: Rational Choice Perspectives on Offending*, New York: Springer-Verlag.

Cornish, D., & Clarke, R. (2003). Opportunities, precipitators and criminal decisions: A reply to Wortley's critique of situational crime prevention. In M. Smith and D. Cornish, eds., *Theory for Practice in Situational Crime Prevention*, vol. 16. Monsey, NY: Criminal Justice Press, pp. 41–96.

Corsaro, N., & Brunson, R. (2013). Are suppression and deterrence mechanisms Enough? Examining the "pulling levers" drug market intervention strategy in Peoria, Illinois, USA. *International Journal of Drug Policy*, 24 (2), 115–121.

Corsaro, N., Brunson, R., & McGarrell, E. (2009). Problem-oriented policing and open-air drug markets: Examining the Rockford pulling levers strategy. *Crime & Delinquency*, 59 (7), 1085–1107.

Corsaro, N., Brunson, R., & McGarrell, E. (2010). Evaluating a policing strategy intended to disrupt an illicit street-level drug market. *Evaluation Review*, 34 (6), 513–548.

Corsaro, N., & Engel, R. (2015). Most challenging of contexts: Assessing the impact of focused deterrence on serious violence in New Orleans. *Criminology & Public Policy*, 14 (3), 471–505.

Corsaro, N., Hunt, E., Hipple, N., & McGarrell, E. (2012). The impact of drug market pulling levers policing on neighborhood violence: An evaluation of the High Point drug market intervention. *Criminology & Public Policy*, 11 (2), 167–199.

Corsaro, N., & McGarrell, E. (2009a). *An Evaluation of the Nashville Drug Market Initiative (DMI) Pulling Levers Strategy*, East Lansing, MI: Michigan State University, School of Criminal Justice.

Corsaro, N., & McGarrell, E. (2009b) Testing a promising homicide reduction strategy: Re-assessing the impact of the Indianapolis "pulling levers" intervention. *Journal of Experimental Criminology*, 5 (1), 63–82.

Cranley, J., Duhaney, P. & Isaac, E. (2020). City's commitment to collaborative agreement stronger than ever. *The Enquirer*, Feb. 21. www.cincinnati.com/story/opinion/2020/02/21/opinion-citys-commitment-collaborative-agreement-stronger-than-ever/4806546002/

Curry, G., Ball, R., & Fox, R. (1994). *Gang Crime and Law Enforcement Record Keeping*, Washington, DC: US National Institute of Justice.

Dalton, E. (2002). Targeted crime reduction efforts in ten communities: Lessons for the project safe neighborhoods initiative. *US Attorney's Bulletin*, 50 (1), 16–25.

Decker, S. (1996). Gangs and violence: The expressive character of collective involvement. *Justice Quarterly*, 11 (2), 231–250.

Delaney, C. (2006). *The Effects of Focused Deterrence on Gang Homicide: An Evaluation of Rochester's Ceasefire Program*, Rochester, NY: Rochester Institute of Technology.

Densley, J., & Squier Jones, D. (2016). Pulling levers on gang violence in London and St. Paul. In Maxson, C. & Esbesnsen, F., eds., *Gang Transitions and Transformations in an International Context*. New York: Springer, pp. 291–305.

Deuchar, R. (2013). *Policing Youth Violence: Transatlantic Connections*, London, UK: IEP Press.

DiIulio, J. (1996). My black crime problem, and ours. *City Journal*, 6 (2), 14–28.

Donovan, J., & Jessor, R. (1985). Structure of problem behavior in adolescence and young adulthood. *Journal of Consulting and Clinical Psychology*, 53 (6), 890–904.

Durlauf, S. & Nagin, D. (2011). Imprisonment and crime: Can both be reduced? *Criminology & Public Policy*, 10 (1), 13–54.

Eberhardt, J. (2019). *Biased: Uncovering the Hidden Prejudiced That Shapes What We See, Think, and Do*, New York: Penguin Books.

Eck, J. (2002). Preventing crime at places. In L. Sherman, D. Farrington, B. Welsh, & D. MacKenzie, eds., *Evidence-based crime prevention*. New York: Routledge, pp. 241–94.

Engel, R., Corsaro, N., & Ozer, M. (2017). The impact of police on criminal justice reform: Evidence from Cincinnati, Ohio. *Criminology & Public Policy*, 16 (2), 375–402.

Engel, R., Corsaro, N., & Skubak Tillyer, M. (2010). *Evaluation of the Cincinnati Initiative to Reduce Violence (CIRV)*, Cincinnati, OH: University of Cincinnati Policing Institute.

Engel, R., Skubak Tillyer, M., & Corsaro, N. (2013). Reducing gang violence using focused deterrence: Evaluating the Cincinnati Initiative to Reduce Violence (CIRV). *Justice Quarterly*, 30 (3), 403–439.

Esbensen, F. & Huizinga, D. (1993). Gangs, drugs, and delinquency in a survey of urban youth. *Criminology*, 31 (4), 565–589.

Fagan, J. (2002). Law, social science, and racial profiling. *Justice Research and Policy*, 4 (1–2), 103–129.

Felson, M. (1986). Routine activities, social controls, rational decisions, and criminal outcomes. In D. Cornish and R. Clarke, eds., *The Reasoning Criminal*. New York: Springer-Verlag, pp. 119–131.

Fox, A., Novak, K., & Yaghoub, M. (2015). *Measuring the Impact of Kansas City's No Violence Alliance*, Kansas City, MO: Department of Criminal Justice and Criminology, University of Missouri – Kansas City.

Frabutt, J., Shelton, T., Di Luca, K., Harvey, L., & Hefner, M. (2009). *A Collaborative Approach to Eliminating Street Drug Markets through Focused Deterrence*, Washington, DC: National Institute of Justice, US Department of Justice.

Goldstein, H. (1990). *Problem-Oriented Policing*, Philadelphia: Temple University Press.

Grasmick, H., & Bursik, R. (1990). Conscience, significant others, and rational choice: Extending the deterrence model. *Law & Society Review*, 24 (3), 837–862

Griffiths, E., & Christian, J. (2015). Considering focused deterrence in the age of Ferguson, Baltimore, North Charleston, and beyond. *Criminology & Public Policy*, 14 (3), 573–581.

Grunwald, B., & Papachristos, A. (2017). Project safe neighborhoods in Chicago: Looking back a decade later. *Journal of Criminal Law and Criminology*, 107 (1), 131–160.

Hamilton, B., Rosenfeld, R., & Levin, A. (2018). Opting out of treatment: Self-selection bias in a randomized controlled study of a focused deterrence notification meeting. *Journal of Experimental Criminology*, 17(1),1–17.

Hawken, A., & Kleiman, M. (2009). *Managing Drug Involved Probationers with Swift and Certain Sanctions: Evaluating Hawaii's HOPE* (No. 229023). Washington, DC: National Institute of Justice.

Heinrich, T., & Braga, A. (2010). *Focused Deterrence and Norm Changing Strategies: The Problem of Sustainability*, New York: National Network for Safe Communities.

High Point Police Department (2014). *Offender Focused Domestic Violence Initiative: The First Two Years*, High Point, NC: High Point Police Department.

Howell, J., & Griffiths, E. (2016). *Gangs in America's Communities*, 2nd edn, Thousand Oaks, CA: Sage.

Jackson, J., & Bradford, B. (2009). Crime, policing and social order: On the expressive nature of public confidence in policing. *British Journal of Sociology*, 60(3),493–521

Jacobs, E., Campanile, C., & Golding, B. (2020) Bloomberg in leaked 2015 clip: '95% of murderers fit one description, Xerox it" *New York Post*, February 11. https://nypost.com/2020/02/11/leaked-bloomberg-audio-shows-him-defending-throw-them-up-against-the-walls-stop-and-frisk/

Jennings, W., Piquero, A., & Reingle, J. (2012). On the overlap between victimization and offending: A review of the literature. *Aggression and Violent Behavior*, 17 (1), 16–26.

Johnson, C. (2014). 20 years later, parts of major crime bill viewed as terrible mistake. *National Public Radio*, September 12. www.npr.org/2014/09/12/347736999/20-years-later-major-crime-bill-viewed-as-terrible-mistake

Jonathan-Zamir, T., & Weisburd, D. (2013). The effects of security threats on antecedents of police legitimacy: Findings from a quasi-experiment in Israel. *Journal of Research in Crime and Delinquency*, 50 (1), 3–32.

Kennedy, D. (1990). *Fighting the Drug Trade in Link Valley*, John F. Kennedy School of Government Case Study C16-90–935.0, Cambridge, MA: Harvard University.

Kennedy, D. (1997). Pulling levers: Chronic offenders, high-crime settings, and a theory of prevention. *Valparaiso University Law Review*, 31 (2): 449–484.

Kennedy, D. (2004). Rethinking law enforcement strategies to prevent domestic violence. *Networks*, 19 (2–3), 8–15.

Kennedy, D. (2019). Policing and the lessons of focused deterrence. In D. Weisburd and A. Braga, eds., *Police Innovation: Contrasting Perspectives*, 2nd edn. New York: Cambridge University Press, pp. 205–226.

Kennedy, D. (2008). *Deterrence and Crime Prevention: Reconsidering the Prospect of Sanction*, London, UK: Routledge Press.

Kennedy, D. (2009a). Drugs, race and common ground: reflections on the High Point intervention. *National Institute of Justice Journal*, 262, 12–17.

Kennedy, D. (2009b). Gangs and public policy: Constructing and deconstructing gang databases. *Criminology & Public Policy*, 8 (4), 711–716.

Kennedy, D. (2011). *Don't shoot: One man, a street fellowship, and the end of violence in inner-city America*, New York: Bloomsbury.

Kennedy, D. (2016). Using the drug market intervention strategy to address the heroin epidemic. *US Attorneys Bulletin*, 64 (5), 19–24.

Kennedy, D., & Friedrich, M. A. (2014). *Custom Notifications: Individualized Communication in the Group Violence Intervention*, Washington, DC: Office of Community Oriented Policing Services.

Kennedy, D., & Ben-Menachem, J. (2019). Moving toward an American police-community reconciliation framework. In T. Lave and E. Miller, eds., *The Cambridge Handbook of Policing in the United States*. New York: Cambridge University Press, pp. 563–580.

Kennedy, D., Braga, A., & Piehl, A. (1997). The (un)known universe: Mapping gangs and gang violence in Boston. In D. Weisburd and J. McEwen, eds., *Crime Mapping and Crime Prevention, Crime Prevention Studies*, vol. 8. Monsey, New York: Criminal Justice Press, pp. 219–262.

Kennedy, D., Braga, A., & Piehl, A. (2001). *Reducing Gun Violence: The Boston Gun Project's Operation Ceasefire*, Washington, DC: US Department of Justice, National Institute of Justice.

Kennedy, D., Kleiman, M., & Braga, A. (2017). Beyond deterrence: Strategies of focus and fairness. In N. Tilley and A. Sidebottom, eds., *Handbook of*

Crime Prevention and Community Safety, 2nd edn. New York: Routledge, pp. 157–182.

Kennedy, D., Piehl, A., & Braga, A. (1996). Youth violence in Boston: Gun markets, serious youth offenders, and a use-reduction strategy. *Law and Contemporary Problems*, 59 (1), 147–196.

Kennedy, D., & Wong, S. (2009). *The High Point Drug Market Intervention Strategy*, Washington, DC: U.S. Department of Justice, Office of Community Oriented Policing Services.

Kirk, D., & Papachristos, A. (2011). Cultural mechanisms and the persistence of neighborhood violence. *American Journal of Sociology*, 116 (4), 1190–1233

Kleck, G., Sever, B., Li, S., & Gertz, M. (2005). The missing link in general deterrence research. *Criminology*, 43 (3), 623–60.

Kleiman, M. (2009). *When Brute Force Fails: How to Have Less Crime and Less Punishment*, Princeton, NJ: Princeton University Press.

Kleiman, M., & Young, R. (1995). The factors of production in retail drug dealing. *Urban Affairs Review*, 30 (5), 730–748.

Klein, M. (1995). *The American Street Gang: Its Nature, Prevalence, and Control*. Oxford University Press.

Klein, M. (2011) Comprehensive gang and violence reduction programs: Reinventing the square wheel. *Criminology & Public Policy*, 10 (4), 1037–1044.

Klofas, J., & Hipple, N. (2006). *Crime Incident Reviews*, Project Safe Neighborhoods: Strategic Interventions Case Study No. 3., Washington, DC: US Department of Justice.

Langford, L., Isaac, N., & Adams, S. (2000). Criminal and restraining order histories of intimate partner-related homicide offenders in Massachusetts, 1991–1995. In P. Blackman, V. Leggett, B. Olson, and J. Jarvis, eds., *The Varieties of Homicide and Its Research: Proceedings of the 1999 Meeting of the Homicide Research Working Group*. Washington, DC: Federal Bureau of Investigation, pp. 57–66.

La Vigne, N., Jannetta, J., Fontaine, J., Lawrence, D., & Esthappan, S. (2019). *The National Initiative for Building Community Trust and Justice: Key Process and Outcome Evaluation Findings*, Washington, DC: Urban Institute.

Leigh, B. (1999). Peril, chance, adventure: Concepts of risk, alcohol use and risky behavior in young adults. *Addiction*, 94 (3), 371–83.

Lipsey, M. & Wilson, D. (2001). *Practical Meta-Analysis*, Thousand Oaks, CA: Sage Publications.

Lisak, D., & Miller, P. (2002). Repeated rape and multiple offending among undetected rapists. *Violence and Victims*, 17 (1), 73–84.

Loughin, E. (2016) Precision policing key to fighting crime. *Irish Examiner*, December 5. www.irishexaminer.com/ireland/ny-precision-policing-key-to-fighting-city-crime-433665.html

Ludwig, J., Kling, J., & Mullainathan, S. (2011). Mechanism experiments and policy evaluations. *Journal of Economic Perspectives*, 25 (3), 17–38.

Lurie, S. (2019). There's no such thing as a dangerous neighborhood. *CityLab*, February 25. www.citylab.com/perspective/2019/02/broken-windows-theory-policing-urban-violence-crime-data/583030/

MacQuarrie, B. (2015). In Rutland, VT, a rare glimmer of hope in battle against opioid addiction. *Boston Globe*, October 26. www.bostonglobe.com/metro/2015/10/26/rutland-makes-gains-opioid-battle/0xJPia7xu1mQDI3jpFUPVK/story.html

Martinez, N., Lee, Y., & Eck, J. (2017). Ravenous wolves revisited: A systematic review of offending concentration. Crime Science, 6 (1). https://doi.org/10.1186/s40163-017-0072-2

Matthews, R. (2014). Rational choice, routine activities and situational crime prevention. In R. Matthews, *Realist Criminology*. London: Palgrave Macmillan, pp. 72–93.

Matza, D. (1964). *Delinquency and Drift*, New Brunswick: Transaction Publishers.

McDonald, P. (2002). *Managing Police Operations: Implementing the New York Crime Control Model – Compstat*, Belmont, CA: Wadsworth.

McGarrell, E., Chermak, S., Wilson, J., & Corsaro, N. (2006). Reducing homicide through a "lever-pulling" strategy. *Justice Quarterly*, 23 (2), 214–229.

McGarrell, E., Corsaro, N., Hipple, N., & Bynum, T. (2010). Project safe neighborhoods and violent crime trends in US cities: Assessing violent crime impact. *Journal of Quantitative Criminology*, 26 (2), 165–190.

McGloin, J. (2005). Policy and intervention considerations of a network analysis of street gangs. *Criminology & Public Policy*, 4 (3), 607–636.

Meares, T. (2009). The legitimacy of police among young African American men. *Marquette Law Review*, 92 (4), 651–666.

Meares, T., & Kahan, D. (1998). Law and (norms of) order in the inner city. *Law and Society Review*, 32 (4), 805–838.

Mentel, Z. (2012). *Racial Reconciliation, Truth-Telling, and Police Legitimacy*, Washington, DC: Office of Community Oriented Policing Services.

Miethe, T. & Meier, R. (1994). *Crime and Its Social Context: Toward an Integrated Theory of Offenders, Victims, and Situations*, New York: State University of New York Press.

Miller, W. (1975). *Violence by Youth Gangs and Youth Groups as a Crime Problem in Major American Cities*, Washington, DC: U.S. Government Printing Office.

Moore, M. (2002). *Recognizing Value in Policing*, Washington, DC: Police Executive Research Forum.

Moore, M., & Braga, A. (2003). Measuring and improving police performance: The lessons of Compstat and its progeny. *Policing: An International Journal of Police Strategies and Management*, 26 (3), 439–453.

Morgan, S. & Winship, C. (2007). *Counterfactuals and Causal Inference: Methods and Principals for Social Research*, New York: Cambridge University Press.

Nagin, D. (2013). Deterrence in the twenty-first century. In M. Tonry, ed., *Crime and Justice: A Review of Research*, vol. 42. Chicago: University of Chicago Press, pp. 199–263.

Nagin, D., & Telep, C. (2017). Procedural justice and legal compliance. *Annual Review of Law and Social Science*, 13 (1), 5–28.

National Network for Safe Communities. (2013). *Group Violence Intervention: An Implementation Guide*, Washington, DC: US Department of Justice, Office of Community Oriented Policing Services.

National Network for Safe Communities (2014). *Drug Market Intervention: An Implementation Guide*, Washington, DC: Office of Community Oriented Policing Services.

National Network for Safe Communities (2015). *Prison Violence Intervention*, New York: John Jay College of Criminal Justice.

National Network for Safe Communities (2016). *Implementing the Drug Market Intervention in Emerging Heroin Markets*, New York: John Jay College of Criminal Justice.

Osgood, W., Johnston, L., O'Malley, P., & Bachman, J. (1988). The generality of deviance in late adolescence and early adulthood. *American Sociological Review*, 53 (1), 81–93.

Padilla, F. (1992). *The Gang as an American Enterprise*, New Brunswick, NJ: Rutgers University Press.

Papachristos, A., Braga, A., & Hureau, D. (2012). Social networks and the risk of gunshot injury. *Journal of Urban Health*, 89 (6), 992–1003.

Papachristos, A., Hureau, D., & Braga, A. (2013). The corner and the crew: The influence of geography and social networks on gang violence. *American Sociological Review*, 78 (3), 417–447.

Papachristos, A., & Kirk, D. (2015). Changing the street dynamic: Evaluating Chicago's group violence reduction strategy. *Criminology & Public Policy*, 14 (3), 525–558.

Papachristos, A., Meares, T., & Fagan, J. (2007). Attention felons: Evaluating project safe neighborhoods in Chicago. *Journal of Empirical Legal Studies*, 4 (2), 223–272.

Papachristos, A., Meares, T., & Fagan, J. (2012). Why do criminals obey the law? The influence of legitimacy and social networks on active gun offenders. *Journal of Criminal Law and Criminology*, 102 (2), 397–440.

Papachristos, A., Wildeman, C., & Roberto, E. (2015). Tragic, but not random: The social contagion of nonfatal gunshot injuries. Social Science & Medicine, 125, 139–150.

Paternoster, R., Brame, R., Bachman, R., & Sherman, L. W. (1997). Do fair procedures matter? The effect of procedural justice on spouse assault. *Law & Society Review*, 31(1),163–204.

Piliavin, I., Thornton, C., Gartner, R., & Matsueda, R. (1986) Crime, deterrence, and rational choice. *American Sociological Review*, 51 (1), 101–119.

Pitts, J. (2007). *Reluctant Gangsters: Youth Gangs in Waltham Forest*, Bedfordshire, UK: University of Bedfordshire.

Reisig, M., Bratton, J., & Gertz, M. (2007). The construct validity and refinement of process-based policing measures. *Criminal Justice and Behavior*, 34 (8), 1005–1028.

Reppetto, T. (1976). Crime prevention and the displacement phenomenon. *Crime & Delinquency*, 22 (2), 166–177.

Roehl, J., Rosenbaum, D., Costello, S., Coldren, J., Schuck, A., Kunard, L., & Forde, D. (2008). *Paving the Way for Project Safe Neighborhoods: SACSI in 10 U.S. Cities*, Washington, DC: US Department of Justice, National Institute of Justice.

Rolph, J., Chaiken, J., & Houchens, R. (1981). *Methods for Estimating the Crime Rates of Individuals*, Santa Monica, CA: RAND Corporation.

Roman, C., Forney, M., Hyatt, J., Klein, H., & Link, N. (2019). Law enforcement activities of Philadelphia's group violence intervention: An examination of arrest, case processing, and probation levers. *Police Quarterly*, https://doi.org/10.1177/1098611119895069

Roman, C., Link, N., Hyatt, J., Bhati, A., & Forney, M. (2019). Assessing the gang-level and community-level effects of the Philadelphia focused deterrence strategy. *Journal of Experimental Criminology*, 15 (4), 499–527.

Rossi, P. (1987). The iron law of evaluation and other metallic rules. *Research in Social Problems and Public Policy*, 4, 3–20.

Rowe, M., & Søgaard, T. (2020). 'Playing the man, not the ball': targeting organised criminals, intelligence and the problems with pulling levers. *Policing and Society*, 30 (2), 120–135.

Sampson, R. (2012). *Great American City: Chicago and the Enduring Neighborhood Effect*, Chicago: University of Chicago Press.

Sampson, R., & Bartusch, D. (1988). Legal cynicism and (subcultural?) tolerance of deviance: The neighborhood context of racial differences. *Law & Society Review*, 32 (4), 777–804.

Sampson, R., Raudenbush, S., & Earls, F. (1997). Neighborhoods and violent crime. *Science*, 277, 918–924.

Saunders, J., Kilmer, B., & Ober, A. (2015). *A Comprehensive Evaluation of a Drug Market Intervention Training Cohort*, Santa Monica, CA: RAND Corporation.

Saunders, J., Lundberg, R., Braga, A., Ridgeway, G., & Miles, J. (2015). A synthetic control approach to evaluating place-based crime interventions. *Journal of Quantitative Criminology*, 31 (3), 413–434.

Saunders, J., Ober, A., Kilmer, B., & Greathouse, S. (2016). *A Community-Based, Focused-Deterrence Approach to Closing Overt Drug Markets: A Process and Fidelity Evaluation of Seven Sites*, Santa Monica, CA: RAND Corporation.

Saunders, J., Robbins, M., & Ober, A. (2017). Moving from efficacy to effectiveness: Implementing the drug market intervention across multiple sites. *Criminology & Public Policy*, 16 (3), 787–814.

Seabrook, J. (2009). Don't shoot: A radical approach to the problem of gang violence. *The New Yorker*, June 22.

Sechrist, S., & Weil, J. (2018). Assessing the impact of a focused deterrence strategy to combat intimate partner domestic violence. *Violence Against Women*, 24 (3), 243–265.

Shaw, C., & McKay, H. (1942). *Juvenile Delinquency in Urban Areas*, Chicago: University of Chicago Press

Sierra-Arévalo, M. (2016). Legal cynicism and protective gun ownership among active offenders in Chicago. *Cogent Social Sciences*, 2 (1), 1227293.

Sierra-Arévalo, M., Charette, Y., & Papachristos, A. (2015). *Evaluating the Effect of Project Longevity on Group-Involved Shootings and Homicides in New Haven, CT*, New Haven, CT: Yale University.

Silverman, E. (1999). *NYPD Battles Crime: Innovative Strategies in Policing*, Boston: Northeastern University Press.

Skogan, W., & Frydl, K, eds. (2004). *Fairness and Effectiveness in Policing: The Evidence*, Committee to Review Research on Police Policy and Practices, Washington, DC: The National Academies Press.

Skubak Tillyer, M., Engel, R. & Lovins, B. (2012). Beyond Boston: Applying theory to understand and address sustainability issues in focused deterrence initiatives for violence reduction. *Crime & Delinquency*, 58 (6), 973–997.

Skubak Tillyer, M., & Kennedy, D. (2008). Locating focused deterrence approaches within a situational crime prevention framework. *Crime Prevention and Community Safety*, 10(2), 75–84.

Spelman, W. (1990). *Repeat Offender Programs*, Washington, DC: Police Executive Research Forum.

Stark, E. (1993). The myth of black violence. *Social Work*, 38 (4), 485–490.

Stuntz, W. (2011). *The Collapse of American Criminal Justice*, Cambridge, MA: Harvard University Press.

Sunshine, J., & Tyler, T. R. (2003). The role of procedural justice and legitimacy in shaping public support for policing. *Law and Society Review*, 37(3),513–548.

Tankebe, J. (2013). Viewing things differently: The dimensions of public perceptions of police legitimacy. *Criminology*, 51(1),103–135.

Thacher, D. (2016). Channeling police discretion: The hidden potential of focused deterrence. *University of Chicago Legal Forum*, http://chicagoun bound.uchicago.edu/uclf/vol2016/iss1/13

The Local. (2019). Malmö pushes ahead with US anti-gang method after shootings, November 13. www.thelocal.se/20191113/malm-police-push-ahead-with-anti-gang-method-despite-shootigs

Tita, G., Riley, K., Ridgeway, G., Grammich, C., Abrahamse, A., & Greenwood, P. (2004). *Reducing Gun Violence: Results from an Intervention in East Los Angeles*, Santa Monica, CA: RAND Corporation.

Travis, J. (1998). Crime, justice, and public policy. Plenary presentation to the American Society of Criminology, Washington, DC, November 12, www .ojp.usdoj.gov/nij/speeches/asc.htm

Trinkner, R. (2019). Addressing the "black box" of focused deterrence: An examination of the mechanisms of change in Chicago's Project Safe Neighborhoods. *Journal of Experimental Criminology*, 15 (4), 673–683.

Turanovic, J., Reisig, M., & Pratt, T. (2015). Risky lifestyles, low self-control, and violent victimization across gendered pathways to crime. *Journal of Quantitative Criminology*, 31 (2), 183–206.

Tyler, T. (2003). Procedural justice, legitimacy, and the effective rule of law. In M. Tonry, ed., *Crime and Justice: A Review of Research*, vol. 30. Chicago: University of Chicago Press, pp. 283–357.

Tyler, T. (2006). *Why People Obey the Law*, 2nd edn, Princeton, N.J.: Princeton University Press.

Tyler, T., Fagan, J., & Geller, A. (2014). Street stops and police legitimacy: Teachable moments in young urban men's legal socialization. *Journal of Empirical Legal Studies*, 11 (4), 751–785.

Tyler, T., Goff, P., & MacCoun, R. (2015). The impact of psychological science on policing in the United States: Procedural justice, legitimacy, and effective law enforcement. *Psychological Science in the Public Interest*, 16 (3), 75–109.

Tyler, T., & Wakslak, C. (2004). Profiling and police legitimacy: Procedural justice, attributions of motive, and acceptance of police authority. *Criminology*, 42(2), 253–282.

Vigil, J. (1988). *Barrio Gangs: Street Life and Identity in Southern California*, Austin: University of Texas Press.

Wallace, D., Papachristos, A., Meares, T., & Fagan, J. (2016). Desistance and legitimacy: The impact of offender notification meetings on recidivism among high risk offenders. *Justice Quarterly*, 33 (1), 1–28.

Warr, M. (2002). *Companions in Crime: The Social Aspects of Criminal Conduct*, New York: Cambridge University Press.

Weisburd, D. (2015). The law of crime concentration and the criminology of place. *Criminology*, 53 (2), 133–157.

Weisburd, D., & Braga, A., eds. (2019). *Police Innovation: Contrasting Perspectives*, 2nd edn, New York: Cambridge University Press.

Weisburd, D., & Eck, J. (2004). What can police do to reduce crime, disorder and fear? *The Annals of the American Academy of Political and Social Science*, 593, 42–65.

Weisburd, D., & Green, L. (1995). Policing drug hot spots: The Jersey City DMA experiment. *Justice Quarterly*, 12 (3), 711–736.

Weisburd, D., Lum, C., & Petrosino, A. (2001). Does research design affect study outcomes in criminal justice? *The Annals of the American Academy of Social and Political Sciences*, 578, 50–70.

Weisburd, D., & Majmundar, M. K., eds. (2018). *Proactive Policing: Effects on Crime and Communities*, Committee on Proactive Policing: Effects on Crime, Communities, and Civil Liberties, Washington, DC: The National Academies Press.

Wellford, C., & Cronin, J. (1999). *An Analysis of Variables Affecting the Clearance of Homicides: A Multistate Study*, Washington, DC: Justice Research and Statistics Association.

Wellford, C., Pepper, J., & Petrie, C., eds. (2005). *Firearms and Violence: A Critical Review*, Committee to Improve Research Information and Data on Firearms, Washington, DC: The National Academies Press.

Wheeler, A., McLean, S., Becker, K., & Worden, R. 2019. Choosing Representatives to Deliver the Message in a Group Violence Intervention. *Justice Evaluation Journal*, 2 (2), 93–117.

Williams, D., Currie, D., Linden, W., & Donnelly, P. (2014). Addressing gang-related violence in Glasgow: A preliminary pragmatic quasi-experimental evaluation of the community initiative to reduce violence (CIRV). *Aggression and Violent Behavior*, 19 (6), 686–691.

Williams, K., & Hawkins, R. (1986). Perceptual research on general deterrence: A critical review. *Law & Society Review*, 20 (4), 545–572.

Wilson, J. Q. (1975). *Thinking about Crime*. New York: Basic Books.

Winship, C. & Berrien, J. (1999). Boston Cops and Black Churches. *The Public Interest*, Summer, 52–68.

Wolfgang, M., Figlio, R., & Sellin, T. (1972). *Delinquency in a Birth Cohort*. Chicago: University of Chicago Press.

Wong, J., Gravel, J. *et al.* (2012). *Effectiveness of Street Gang Control Strategies: A Systematic Review and Meta-analysis of Evaluation Studies*, Ottawa, CA: Public Safety Canada.

Wood, G., & Papachristos, A. (2019). Reducing gunshot victimization in high-risk social networks through direct and spillover effects. *Nature Human Behaviour*, 3, 1164–1170.

Worden, R., & McLean, S. (2017). *Mirage of Police Reform: Procedural Justice and Police Legitimacy*, Oakland, CA: University of California Press.

Wright, R., &. Decker, S. (1997) *Armed Robbers in Action: Stickups and Street Culture*, Boston: Northeastern University Press

Zimring, F. (1981). Kids, groups, and crime: Some implications of a well-known secret. *Journal of Criminal Law and Criminology*, 72 (3), 867–885.

Zimring, F., & Hawkins, G. (1973). *Deterrence: The Legal Threat in Crime Control*, Chicago: University of Chicago Press.

Cambridge Elements ≡

Elements in Criminology

David Weisburd

Department of Criminology, Law and Society, George Mason University; Institute of Criminology, Faculty of Law, The Hebrew University of Jerusalem
David Weisburd is Distinguished Professor at George Mason University, and Walter E. Meyer Professor of Law and Criminal Justice at the Hebrew University. He is the recipient of many international awards for his contributions to criminology, including the Stockholm Prize in Criminology, the Israel Prize, and the Sutherland and Vollmer Awards from the American Society of Criminology.

Advisory Board

About the Series

Elements in Criminology seeks to identify key contributions in theory and empirical research that help to stake out advances in contemporary criminology. Rather than summarizing traditional theories and approaches, *Elements in Criminology* seeks to advance "turning points" in recent years, and to identify new turning points as they emerge. The series seeks a mix of forward-looking analytical reviews, as well as reports on innovative new research.

Cambridge Elements ☰

Elements in Criminology

Elements in the Series

Developmental Criminology and the Crime Decline
Jason L. Payne & Alex R. Piquero

A full series listing is available at: www.cambridge.org/ECRM

Printed in the United States
by Baker & Taylor Publisher Services